Tips and Traps for Making Money in Real Estate

Other McGraw-Hill Books by Robert Irwin

TIPS AND TRAPS WHEN BUYING A HOME

TIPS AND TRAPS WHEN SELLING A HOME

TIPS AND TRAPS WHEN MORTGAGE HUNTING

BUY, RENT, & HOLD: HOW TO MAKE MONEY IN A "COLD" REAL ESTATE MARKET

HOW TO FIND HIDDEN REAL ESTATE BARGAINS, REVISED FIRST EDITION

THE MCGRAW-HILL REAL ESTATE HANDBOOK, SECOND EDITION

Tips and Traps for Making Money in Real Estate

Robert Irwin

McGraw-Hill, Inc.

New York   San Francisco   Washington, D.C.   Auckland   Bogotá
Caracas   Lisbon   London   Madrid   Mexico City   Milan
Montreal   New Delhi   San Juan   Singapore
Sydney   Tokyo   Toronto

Library of Congress Cataloging-in-Publication Data

Irwin, Robert.
    Tips and traps for making money in real estate / Robert Irwin
        p.   cm.
    Includes index.
    ISBN 0-07-032383-6 (hard)   —ISBN 0-07-032384-4 (pbk.)
    1. Real estate investment. I. Title.
    HD1382.5.I76   1993
    92-46320   332.63'24—dc20
                                                 CIP

1 2 3 4 5 6 7 8 9 0 DOC/DOC 9 9 8 7 6 5 4 3

ISBN 0-07-032383-6 (HC)
ISBN 0-07-032384-4 (PBK)

*The sponsoring editor for this book was James Bessent, the editing supervisor
was Jim Halston, and the production supervisor was Donald F. Schmidt. It
was set in Palatino by McGraw-Hill's Professional Book Group composition
unit.*

Printed and bound by R. R. Donnelley & Sons Company.

This book is printed on recycled, acid-free paper containing a minimum of 50% recycled de-
inked fiber.

Contents

Preface

The Day of the Small Investor?

This book is written with the small investor in mind, a person who might buy another home (in addition to a personal residence) and rent it out hoping to sell later on for a profit. (If you're in real estate acquisition or disposal for a large corporation, you will still find many of the chapters useful.) If you've invested in a house or apartment building or other property in the past, or are contemplating doing so in the future, this book is for you. The real question is, however, are you for this market?

There was a time not all that long ago when all you had to do to make money in real estate was buy property, almost any property, wait a year or two, and sell. That was it. No brains, no work, no headaches.

Times have changed.

Today, there's still money to be made in real estate, probably more than before. There are still countless opportunities for the small investor who wants to buy a single house, condo, co-op, or other property. And, amazingly, the investment required remains relatively small. Real estate still offers the single greatest road to wealth for the average person in the United States.

But to make money in real estate today requires savvy. You need to know *what* to buy, *where* to buy it, *how much* to pay, and *when* to sell. In short, what's changed is not the method—it still involves purchasing small properties. What's new is the decision-making process.

Today not all properties are good investments. Perhaps not even half of all properties will earn a reasonable profit after five years. Probably less than a fourth of all properties will make you only marginally more money than you might get from stocks, bonds, or even a high-yielding money market account. And, I would guess, less than 10 percent of all properties will get you really big bucks, the doubling of your money and more, when you sell.

The goal of this book is to separate the wheat from the chaff when it comes to real estate. It's to give you the knowledge to pick out that one property in ten that will double or further increase your investment.

In addition, this book will point out the minefield of catastrophes that could await you if you make the wrong move. And it will indicate the right moves to make, and when to make them.

In short, this fourth in the series of *Tips & Traps* books will show you how to invest successfully and make money in today's real estate market.

Robert Irwin

Introduction—
What Makes Money,
What Doesn't

My father, years ago before he passed on, used to speak of real estate as a "money tree." "You should take your money," he would say, and "plant it" in real estate. Then all you had to do was apply "water" (pay the mortgage and taxes), "trim" occasionally (get rid of bad tenants), and "harvest." The latter meant selling or refinancing every so often to get money out after the property had appreciated in value.

From his perspective of two or three decades ago, it really didn't matter where or what you bought. All ground was equally fertile, all "real estate money trees" would grow and yield strong crops.

Perhaps he was right, for his era. But for those who invest today, operating under this sort of analogy can spell disaster. Today, not all real estate investments grow. Many spend years lying dormant. Others simply wither and die.

This is not to say that there is no money to be made in real estate investing. Quite to the contrary, most of the advantages always available in real estate investments remain: high profits, in selected markets; leverage obtained from putting in a relatively small amount of your own money and borrowing the balance; and even tax advantages, if you happen to be at the right income level.

What's different is that today not all properties will make money. In today's market, real estate is like investing in stocks, commodities, rare coins, or anything else: The results can be varied. Some properties will be profitable. Some properties will simply sit there and not appreciate

1

very much in value. And some will go down in value. The trick, of course, is to invest only in properties that make money.

In this chapter we are going to look at a series of clues that should lead you to profitable properties. We'll begin with that old bugaboo, location.

Locate Properties That Make Money

If you've attended seminars or read many investment books in the field, you've probably come to realize that most of the "gurus" and authors tend to tell you the same truth (one that you could quickly discover for yourself): When it comes to buying great properties, go for location, location, location.

One would think that all you had to do to make money today was to identify a good location, buy *any* house, apartment, or commercial building in the area, and start counting your money on the way to the bank.

I'm afraid it just isn't so, anymore.

Yes, location is critical. But location no longer means buying only in the most expensive and best area of town. Today you can often profit more from buying a property in a "lesser" location, but one that is well priced.

Today "location" is more a matter of avoiding a negative feature than zeroing in on a positive one. You want to *avoid* a bad location. However, once you've found a location that isn't bad, the most important thing you need to watch out for is the "price point."

Tip

Think of selling when you buy.

Buying real estate investments to hold indefinitely can be a big mistake for many small investors. Most such purchasers simply don't have a clear plan for selling. Thus, when prices do go up and they can sell at a profit, they continue to hang on. I can't begin to number the real estate investors I know who simply buy and buy and never sell.

In today's real estate market, what goes up also comes down. As soon as any property you have shows a profit, consider selling. With the market as fickle as it is, to hold indefinitely may just mean waiting for the next downturn.

Avoid Negative Cashflows

In today's market, try to avoid properties that have a negative cashflow. The reason is that you may guess wrong and instead of buying a good property, buy a bad one that you can't soon sell for profit. That means you may have to hang on to it for an extended period of time. If the property pays for itself, you should be able to hang on to it virtually forever. However, if the property has a negative cashflow and you have to put money into it each month, you'll soon tire and sell, probably for a loss.

Trap

Beware of no-money-down deals in today's market. The property that doesn't require much cash to get into usually requires you to make substantial monthly payments out of your pocket, and that means negative cashflow. To make a profit, this property demands that you resell quickly. If you aren't able to, it will turn into an "alligator" that will eat up both your financial and your emotional resources.

Pay Attention to the "Price Point"

The term *price point* will be well known to anyone who is involved in consumer retailing. It means that magical price above which consumers will not perceive value, and hence will not buy. For example, the price point in camcorders, a recent consumer electronic marvel, originally was close to $2,000. If a manufacturer brought out a unit that cost more than that magic number, it wouldn't sell. Anything below, did.

However, more and more manufacturers introduced ever more powerful models at lower prices. Thus, consumers began to perceive value at ever lower levels. The price point quickly dropped to around $1,500, then $1,200, then $1,000. As this is being written, my friends in consumer electronics tell me that the price point for a camcorder is roughly $800! By that they mean that any unit priced below that number will quickly sell. Any unit priced higher will sit unsold on the shelves for months. (This doesn't mean that a unit priced higher won't ever sell. It just means that it will take longer, or will need to have special features not found on the lower-priced models.)

These days, the same holds true in real estate. Every area has a price point. Houses above that number simply aren't selling. Those below it are going fast, regardless of the market.

Tip

_____

The quickest way to find a property that will make money, whether it be house, apartment building, or commercial building, is to first identify the price point in your area and, second, to buy well below that point.

Identifying the Price Point

In virtually every area of the country, real estate agents, usually through their professional organizations, compile statistics on sales. Call up an agent and ask to see those statistics. (Most will readily make them available to you, hoping that you will buy through them.) What you want to see is the number of houses sold monthly at given price levels. Note: You may end up with a list of home sales that will require you to categorize them by the number sold and available for each price group.

Here is what a typical breakdown might look like for a local area:

Sales levels at different prices

Number of homes sold	Number of homes available	Sales price range
0	0	$0–25,000
7	11	25,000–50,000
9	20	50,000–60,000
15	35	60,000–70,000
19	40	70,000–80,000
23	63	80,000–90,000
17	79	90,000–100,000
24	73	100,000–110,000
19	83	110,000–120,000
8	71	120,000–130,000
9	89	130,000–140,000
5	69	140,000–150,000
5	53	150,000–160,000
7	37	160,000–170,000
3	41	170,000–180,000
1	39	180,000–190,000
1	23	190,000–200,000
8	19	Over 200,000

Can you identify the price point from this chart? It is $120,000.

The vast majority of home sales are in the price range below $120,000. Relatively few sell above that number. Yet more houses are offered for sale above the price point than below. (Note: There are relatively few sales below $60,000, but that's only because, in the market shown, there are relatively few homes for sale in that price range.)

If we add up the homes for sale and those sold above and below the price point, we end up with the following statistics:

Total houses for sale above price point	441
Total houses for sale below price point	404
Total houses sold above price point	47
Total houses sold below price point	133
Percent of houses sold above price point	11%
Percent of houses sold below price point	33%

The statistics make the point. If you have a house that is above the price point, your chance of selling in the market shown is roughly 11 percent. If you have a house below the price point, your chance of selling is three times higher, 33 percent.

To buy a house that makes money, therefore, identify the price point in your area. Make sure that no matter how much you pay for your home, you will be able to resell it *below* the price point.

Tip

The price point in your area will not remain inflexible. It will tend to rise or fall with supply and demand of housing, and with the ups and downs of the local economy.

Trap

Avoid great locations with homes that are above the price point.

This is the downside to the advice of paying attention only to location, location, location. You may have a great house in a great location, but if it's above the price point, it won't sell. (See Chapter 1 for more information on this.)

Tip

The price point is a critical number. If your property happens to be priced just $500 above it, you risk having a property that won't resell. To make money, be sure to buy well below the price point.

If You're New to the Field, or Work at It Part-Time, Stick with Single-Family Houses

Once you've learned about price point, the next big tip is to stay with single-family housing (SFH). The greatest opportunity in real estate for the individual small investor, particularly one new to the field, remains with single-family homes. Single-family homes are the easiest to rent, the easiest to maintain (provided you don't buy an older home—see below), and offer the best tax advantages currently available.

The truth of the matter is that when it comes time to rent, tenants will look first for single-family homes, then for condos, and only lastly for apartments. Their reasoning has to do with the increased privacy a single-family home offers, with the additional yard space and garage space usually found with such a home, and with the increased size often found in such a property. Thus, you ensure yourself of the largest possible tenant base with a SFH.

Tip

When buying an investment home, it's important to remember the One Percent Rule. This rule simply states that in order to have a profitable property, you should be able to charge one percent of your purchase price as your monthly rental rate. Thus, if your purchase price is $100,000, in order to cover all your payments and show a profit you should be able to rent the property for $1,000 a month. Conversely, if you can rent the property for a maximum of $1,000 a month, you shouldn't pay more than $100,000. If you can stick close to the one percent rule, you won't go far wrong in any single-family housing investment you make.

Trap

In recent years prices, particularly on both coasts, have increased to the point where it has become virtually impossible to buy a home within the parameters of the one percent rule. On the west coast, for example, it will often cost $200,000 to purchase a home that can then be rented for a maximum of only $1,000 a month. In talking with investors I have found many who, as a result, have simply thrown the one percent rule out the window.

That's a great mistake. You can indeed disregard the one percent rule, *if* you can quickly resell. But in recent times reselling has often proved elusive, particularly in a market where prices have declined rather than increased. To disregard the rule means that you end up with a negative cashflow, sometimes a significant one, that may not be overcome by any possible tax write-off for depreciation.

Another advantage of single-family housing is ease of reselling. Although there are exceptions, the general rule is that when the market gets bad, single-family homes will sell faster than condos. Those who own condos are often "stuck," unable to dispose of their property.

Buy Either Few or Many Properties

My next suggestion is that you buy either one or two single-family residences as investments, or buy 20 or more (or an apartment building with at least 20 rentals).

My reasoning here is simple. You can personally manage a few single-family homes. However, you probably can't adequately take care of more than that. And you need about 20 units in order to be able to afford to hire a competent part- or full-time professional management person to take care of them for you.

I know that many longtime investors will pooh-pooh this, saying that they've personally handled as many as a dozen single-family rentals and/or small apartment houses with six or eight units, and have had no problems doing so.

Yes, it can be done. I've done it myself.

But unless you plan to make real estate your full-time job, don't think you can do it well or easily. It's the rare property that doesn't require the landlord to be occasionally taking care of a maintenance or tenant problem. Multiply that by half a dozen or more properties and, in a bad month, you can have your phone ringing every day with complaints and with demands that you get something done.

In the short run, and once in a while, most people can easily handle it. But month after month and year after year the problems wear you down, until you may find yourself doing what a friend of mine finally did when a tenant called at ten at night to complain about a leaking toilet. She told the tenant to, "take that blamed toilet and stick it up your nose!"

Needless to say, the tenant stopped paying rent and, shortly thereafter, moved out.

If you have only one or two rental properties, chances are the problems that arise will be spaced far enough apart that you can easily handle them, both financially and emotionally.

Tip

If you have only a couple of properties, take care of them yourself. With only one or two rentals, you can be right on top of it and get good tenants. You'll save money on almost all costs.

Trap

If you're a small investor with only a few properties, avoid real estate management companies, when possible. It's not that they don't do a good job. Most do. However, those who do good work tend to charge a lot for it. Ten percent of monthly income (whether the place is rented or not) is not atypical. And that's over and above any costs for maintenance, eviction, and other problems. You could easily see your entire month's income in rents go out the window in costs, and not just once in a while but for many months in a row.

On the other hand, if you have 20 or more units, you usually can afford to hire a management company, or perhaps even one person, to manage (and do minor maintenance for) all of your properties as either a full-time or part-time job. Again, have few or many rentals.

Buy Close to Home

If you're going to own a few rental houses and take care of them yourself, then you absolutely must buy close to home. Nothing will make your life more miserable than to attempt to take care of a rental property at a distance. I know; I've tried, and didn't like it one bit.

A number of years ago I was living in Los Angeles and saw the opportunity to obtain a couple of rental houses in a neighboring state, Arizona. I purchased them in Phoenix, which was really only about a 45-minute ride away, by air. By car it took considerably longer.

I hired a small management firm to do the basic renting up of the properties, and figured that when it came to maintenance and repairs I would either hire inexpensive "handymen" or handle the work myself. My anticipations were for an easy ownership and big payday down the road. I was sadly mistaken.

The Phoenix market at the time was overbuilt. (Phoenix, it would seem, has been overbuilt for several decades.) That meant that although I was able to rent the properties, tenants tended to be flighty. They would often leave when another landlord offered a better deal. The result was a lot of cleanup and rerenting.

Added to this were the problems that naturally occurred in an area with a very hot climate. The air conditioning tended to go out. The swimming pool filled with algae, and the pumping system broke down and needed cleaning. The composition shingle roof tended to "wilt" or have the shingles turn up at the ends and leak.

All of these could have been easily remedied had I been close at hand and able to either do it myself or find someone who could handle it as an odd job. However, because I was at a distance, I was forced to rely on the management firm most of the time. And they simply called in professionals who charged top dollar.

As a result, I found myself darting back and forth by air between Los Angeles and Phoenix, sometimes several times a month, trying to keep the properties' expenses down. However, soon the air fares and car rentals alone were eating up much of my rental income. The hired-out repairs and maintenance took the remainder. In short, the properties were alligators; they consistently lost money.

Tip

There's an old rule in real estate that goes by many different names, but I prefer to call it, "Dump the dog." It simply means that if you have a property that isn't producing, get rid of it. The rule, quite simply, is that you are usually throwing good money after bad, if you attempt to prop up a property that for one reason or another cannot sustain itself with at least a "breakeven." The best solution is often a quick end. Get rid of the property even at a loss, accept your knocks, and move on.

I sold the properties in Phoenix. However, because I wasn't able to wait for an opportune time in the market, I was not able to get top dollar. I didn't lose money, but I didn't make money either. And in any business, when you spend time and capital and end up not making money, that's a loss.

The message of this little tale is that the problems were caused, in my opinion, entirely by the distance between myself and the properties. If I could have been right there, I could have handled renting and cleanup by myself. I could have found more economical means to take care of maintenance and repair. I could have avoided spending large amounts of money on traveling.

If you are considering the purchase of investment real estate, I strongly urge you to buy close to home. If possible, buy in your own neighborhood. If not, buy within 5 or 10 miles. Here are some of the advantages of buying close to home:

1. *Easy rent-up.* You can receive inquiries on your home phone, and can quickly get to the property to show it to prospective tenants.
2. *Close tenant contact.* If the tenant is late in paying, a check bounces, the tenant doesn't leave as agreed, or some problem arises, you can be at the property in minutes to deal with the situation.
3. *Simple maintenance.* If a faucet leaks, you can get over there after your regular work and fix it. If a water heater goes out, you can select a new one at the most beneficial price and arrange to have someone install it, again at a good price for you.
4. *Best judgment for repairs.* If a roof goes out, or an air conditioner, you can be on the spot to determine just what's wrong and what is the best and least expensive method of correcting the problem.
5. *Inexpensive cleanup.* If a tenant moves out, you can do the cleanup yourself or hire an inexpensive cleaning service to do it for you.
6. *No unnecessary expenses.* You don't have to pay for travel costs. You don't have to pay for a management service. You don't have to pay someone else to do what you should be doing yourself.

Trap

Most rental properties these days do not produce a large positive cashflow. In fact, the best you can usually hope for is a breakeven. Thus, the amount that you save by being close to the property and handling much of the work yourself can be the difference between a producing property and an alligator.

Buy Newer Properties

This is a suggestion that immediately calls up exceptions, so let's deal with them first. Across the country, investors are buying up thousands of old properties, renovating them, and reselling them at a profit. In fact, in some areas the only properties on which profits can be made are the older ones.

Having said that, however, let's understand that unless you are a home renovator, your goal is to purchase and then resell a property without having to do an enormous amount of work on it. Older properties require work, lots of work.

I once did an informal study of the age at which properties begin to require increasing amounts of repairs and maintenance, by talking with real estate management brokers, particularly those who manage 100 or more properties on a regular basis. The consensus was that properties begin to require some increased maintenance costs at just 7 years of age (water heaters, carpeting, painting, etc.)! Interestingly, they required major maintenance beginning at only about 15 years of age (new roofs, refurbished exteriors, problems with heating/cooling systems, etc).

Thus, my conclusion was that, if possible, if your goal is a quickly resalable investment home that doesn't require a lot of refurbishing, it pays to invest in a younger one, preferably one that is less than 15 years old and if possible, less than 7 years. If you buy anything older than that, you had best be sure that the previous owner has done the required maintenance work.

Trap

In most cases with houses that are under 15 years of age, the previous owner has *not* done much maintenance work. Homeowners typically will put off everything they can that costs money. While they may have replaced a water heater (because they couldn't live in the house without hot water), chances are they won't have redone the roof or repaired the heating or cooling system. What they may have done amounts to just cosmetics. Thus, when you buy at or near the upper age limit noted above (close to 15 years old), you may be getting a home that's just ripe for major costly work.

Tip

You *may* be able to pass on the work to the next buyer. However, it would be foolish to count on it. Yes, sometimes a roof can be patched for a few hundred dollars and it will last a few more years. On the other hand, when you are finally forced to do the work, you may find it will take many thousands to replace that roof.

Yet another reason for getting a new house has to do with the new laws coming on-line in most states with regard to disclosures. Currently, in California, Maine, and a couple of other states, you are required to disclose to a buyer any defects, problems, or faults in a house that you are selling. In addition, these days buyers almost universally have a building inspection to ferret out any problems with a house. And some locales even require a building inspection by a local building department, pursuant to any sale!

The point here is that if you have a newer house, there are going to be fewer problems to be found and disclosed. That means the sale itself will be quicker, cleaner, and less costly. (Problems, if they are correctable, must usually be fixed at the seller's expense.)

If you have an older house, chances are there are going to be all sorts of things that need fixing. Sometimes the cost of fixing them can be astronomical. A friend recently sold a house that was 35 years old. As part of the sale, inspections revealed that the old galvanized steel plumbing was simply worn out and leaking. There were so many leaks it couldn't be fixed, but instead had to be replaced entirely. In addition, the electrical wiring was just as badly off and had to be replaced. It cost her $8,500 to have the house replumbed and rewired. A newer house wouldn't have had either of those problems.

Trap

Sometimes you can be held responsible for failing to disclose information about which you had no knowledge! For example, in Los Angeles recently a couple bought an older home from an investor. The investor had owned the property for only a little over a year. He disclosed all that he knew about the home, which wasn't much since he had rented it out, not lived in it during his ownership.

The new owners moved in and discovered from neighbors that a couple of years earlier a woman had committed suicide in the home. They claimed that their ethnic and religious upbringing made it a taboo to live in a house in which a suicide had occurred. They sued the seller for recision of the deal—and won! The seller had to take back the house, repay them their money, plus pay penalties, all because he hadn't disclosed the suicide, which he didn't even know about! (See Chapter 6, which points out inspection pitfalls.)

Get a Shorter-Term, Lower-Interest-Rate Mortgage

We'll have a lot more to say on mortgages in a separate chapter. However, one point worth making strongly is that it often pays to sacrifice length of term in order to get a mortgage that has a significantly lower interest rate. The lower interest rate, and consequently lower monthly payment, often can make the difference between a property that has a positive cashflow and one that costs money out of pocket to maintain each month.

There are two ways to trade off a reduced term into a lower interest rate. The first is to go for a straight short-term mortgage. For example, if you opt for a 15-year mortgage, you can often get somewhere around a one-percent lower interest rate than you would with a straight 30-year mortgage. The good news is that you'll end up paying a lower overall amount in interest. The bad news is that the shorter term means that your monthly payments, even though the interest portion of them will be less, may be higher overall. (Paying off in 15 years requires about a 15 percent higher mortgage payment than if you were paying off in 30 years.)

The other alternative is a 30-year term with a balloon payment. Currently these are available with the balloon due in years 3, 5, 7, or 10. The shorter the balloon payment, the lower the mortgage interest. For a 3- or 5-year balloon payment, the mortgage interest rate could be a percent lower than for a straight 30-year loan with no balloon. (A balloon payment means that at a certain point, the entire mortgage becomes due. For example, a 7-year balloon means that although the mortgage payments are spread out over 30 years, after 7 years the mortgage becomes fully due and payable.)

Going for a 30-year mortgage with a short balloon is likely to get you both the lowest monthly payment and the lowest interest rate. (Note: In some cases these loans may be limited to only those who intend to buy properties in which they plan to live. If that's the case, you might want to buy the property, live in it for a year or more, and then convert it to a rental. See Chapter 5 for more details and cautions.)

Tip

It's vital that you estimate how long you're going to be holding the property before you get a short balloon. If you are confident of a quick resell, then you may want to opt for the shortest three-year term. It typically offers the fewest costs (lowest points) and lowest interest rate.

If, however, you are unsure of how long you will need to keep the property, you may still get a lower-interest-rate balloon, but with the longest possible term, typically 10 years. These longer balloon mortgages are not so readily available, and you'll have to search for them. Also, they often cost more in points and have a slightly higher interest rate than their shorter-balloon-term cousins. Yet they buy peace of mind, by allowing you to know that you have a full decade in which to resell for a profit.

Contrary to widespread belief, these balloon/30-year mortgages do not always carry a "bail-out" clause in them. That means they don't necessarily convert to some other type of mortgage. Thus when the balloon is due, and if you can't resell, you could be in trouble if you can't refinance. However, often for a small additional charge at the time you get the mortgage (usually a quarter to half a point), you can buy a "bail-out" clause. This allows you to automatically convert the mortgage to an adjustable rate at the time the balloon is due.

To my thinking, this extra cost is worthwhile as a "just in case" relief valve.

For the Daring, There Are Apartment and Commercial Buildings

On the other hand, there's a great deal of money to be made at the present time in both apartments and commercial buildings. But the risks are commensurately great.

In order to consider these types of investments, my feeling is that you must have the following three ingredients:

1. *Substantial capital.* You will need enough to put a strong down payment into the property and to keep you afloat for at least six months, or until you can get the property fully rented up.

2. *Time.* These properties in today's market are not going to take care of themselves. They require lots of personal attention. Further, it's unlikely you will be able to find someone to do the work for you. Thus, it's entirely up to you. If you have a full-time regular job, forget this kind of investment. You simply don't have the time for it.

3. *Risk-taking ability.* Today, many apartment buildings are either rundown and require extensive fix-up work, or are overpriced. Commercial buildings are overbuilt everywhere, and require special handling in order to fill them with rent-paying tenants. All this means that the chance for failure is at least as high as that for success. If you don't take risks well, don't apply here.

Apartment buildings used to be the darlings of the real estate investor. You bought the property, jacked up the rents, and, because price is figured as a multiple of rents, resold for a stunning profit.

Over the years, however, so many investors have done this that many, if not most, apartment buildings, already have rents maxed out. Thus, today when you buy an apartment building you risk paying top dollar. You might have to keep the building for many years before you could raise rents to the point where you could sell for a significant profit.

Trap

The often unmentioned problem with apartment buildings is rent control. Because so many investors raised rents so fast in the past (in order to resell at a profit), many jurisdictions have imposed rent controls on buildings with four or more units. While investors often raised rents recklessly, without regard for tenants' abilities to pay, rent controls often bend too far the other way by preventing owners from raising rents even when they may need to raise money for maintenance or other required costs. If you buy an apartment building in a rent control area, you had better be sure that you have sufficient positive cashflow to make the investment worthwhile. The chances of your reselling for a profit anytime in the near future are usually very small.

The greatest risks, and potentially the greatest rewards, in today's market are in commercial buildings. The latter were enormously overbuilt during the 1980s. As of this writing, vacancy rates in some areas approach 25 percent or more. (Five to nine percent is often considered a normal vacancy rate.)

It could take until the year 2,000, or longer, for demand to rise to meet current supply in some areas.

Tip

Perhaps the best investments available in real estate today are commercial buildings. As noted, they are overbuilt everywhere and, as a result, are difficult to rent. Many are in foreclosure. As of this writing, many are still owned by the Resolution Trust Corporation.

However, that means that prices are often ridiculously low. Those hardy entrepreneurs who buy such properties often get them for fire sale prices. If they are then rented out ruthlessly to pay the operational costs, and kept until the market eventually turns around (which could take five years or more), the profits could be astronomical.

BIG Tip

Big investors, those who either individually or in groups can come up with 3 to 5 million dollars in cash, are making money "hand over fist" in today's commercial building market. One such group I know of put together $5 million, then borrowed an additional $17 million to purchase a 43-million-dollar property from the Resolution Trust Corporation. (That's right, the RTC was so desperate to get rid of the property it sold a $43-million property for $22 million!) The group then sold off half the property for $22 million to another investor group, paid back their entire financing as well as their entire capital investment, and now still owns a 21-million-dollar performing commercial property, free and clear!

You can get information on RTC properties by calling direct. Check with 800-information for current numbers. You can also very likely get information on other foreclosed commercial properties simply by contacting any large bank or savings and loan in your area.

In this chapter we've looked at some big tips and clues on how to make money in real estate in a general way. In the following chapter, we'll get down to specifics.

1

Plan Ahead—
Sell Before
You Buy

How do you make money in real estate, today?

The answer is that you do it the old-fashioned way. You buy low and sell high. What's implied is that in order to make money you will have to sell.

Although the above should almost be a truism, there are many who will strongly disagree. They feel that the way to make money in real estate is to buy properties, a lot of them, and then hang on to them "forever," having the rental income slowly pay them off. Hold the properties for 30 years or until they are free and clear, they advocate, and live off the rental income. When you want cash, simply refinance.

Their goal is admirable. (I even wrote a book that touches on this subject, *Buy, Rent, and Hold*, McGraw-Hill, 1991, in which I suggest that you hold properties until a market turnaround occurs.) In this current book, however, I am advocating a different approach, that of buying and selling in a relatively short time. There are a number of reasons for this new approach.

1. The market has become erratic. In the old days, prices went in only one direction—up. Today they go both ways. For any given house in any given market, over a decade, chances are the prices will be up part of the time and down another part. Thus, real estate today is more like stocks and bonds. To win you need to play the market—buy on the dips, sell on the spikes.

2. Neighborhoods are changing faster. You may buy a property in a great location, but a decade later it may be in a slum.

3. As properties age, the number of problems with them increases to the point where, by the time the property is 30 years old, you can be spending many thousands of dollars a year on upkeep and renovation. Even though the property may have been fairly new when you bought it, hold it long enough and it becomes old and broken-down.

4. Recent changes in the tax code (passive activity losses) make holding properties far less advantageous than in the past, particularly for those with higher incomes. Many people cannot write off their losses until they sell. (See Chapter 12.)

For these reasons, I feel that to make money on property today, a good approach is to have a goal of making a quick profit. This isn't to say that you can't hold a property until the market turns around, even if it takes several years. Or that you can't hold for a long time, say 10 years, when you have a positive cashflow. It's just that, when possible, a quick profit may be more advantageous than hanging on for a long time for more money.

Tip

You make your profit when you buy, not when you sell. This simply means that in order to sell right, you have to buy right. Pay too much, and you'll never make money when you sell. Pay a good low price, and selling will be easy and profitable.

Buying Right

When it comes time to buy a piece of property, *foremost* in your mind should be the question, "What can I sell this for?" In other words, you should be thinking about reselling *before* you buy. If you wait until afterward, it could be too late.

Thinking about reselling early on focuses you on just how much you really can afford to pay for a property. Naturally we all want to buy inexpensively. But "inexpensive" is relative. A property may seem cheap compared to what other homes are listed for. But when compared to what you can resell for, given the costs of reselling (commission, escrow, title, etc.), it may not be inexpensive at all.

Often those who are new to this field are astonished at how low the maximum amount they can afford to pay for a home today is, in order to sell it profitably tomorrow. Oftentimes it is more than 25 percent less than the asking price!

Trap

Don't wait for prices to go up. In the old days, all you had to do was buy any property and sit back and wait. Inflation-driven price increases of 5 to 10 percent a year would ensure that you could resell for a profit in as little as two years' time, even if you had originally bought at market price.

That isn't the case anymore in most areas. Houses today may sit with their prices unchanged for many years. In some cases, they may go down in value. (See Chapter 2, for more on buying in a depressed market.) Thus, you can't count on appreciation to bail out your investment. Rather, you have to find a true bargain when you buy.

As noted, buying right means that the question foremost in your mind at the time of buying must be, "What can I sell this property for?" However, saying this to yourself and actually getting the property at the necessary price (for you to make a profit) can be two very different things.

Let's take an example. You go out with an agent and look at a variety of homes. You have told the agent that you're interested in buying an investment property. You anticipate you might have to hold it a year or two. You might have to do cleanup, fix-up work. But beyond that what you're looking for is something that you can get cheaply so you can sell for a profit.

Chances are the agent will inform you that you're not the only one on the block looking for a "steal." She may say that everyone wants to "steal" a piece of property, but there just aren't many "steals" out there. If there were, she or other buyers would have picked them up.

Then she may show you a series of houses that are "priced right" or "priced to sell." These may be homes that are at or close to the price other similar homes recently sold for.

The implication is that there's something wrong with you if you want to buy cheaply. You're not an entrepreneur or a business person, you're a thief, hence the word "steal" tends to come up a lot in these situations.

Further, you are then shown homes that are "good buys," or at least good for someone who wants a place to live. You are then expected to make an offer on one or more of these. The implication is that this is the way the system operates and in order to move forward, you'll just have to do as everyone else does. Find a "good" house and make an offer. Then sit on it for a while (like they used to do in the old days) until it's gone up enough for you to list it for sale. If that time period happens to be 20 years, well, that's way it goes.

If you are bullied into making an offer and buying an investment house on this basis, chances are you lose. The reason is simple. You're buying at retail. You're paying the shelter cost of the house, not the investment price. It may indeed take many years or more for you to get your money back out. And during that time, unless you've bought very carefully, the house could be costing you money out-of-pocket every month.

Looking More Deeply

The truth of the matter is that you probably won't find a good *investment* house by simply going out with the average agent and perusing what's available through the Multiple Listings. (This isn't to say you won't find a good home in which to live. You almost certainly will. But here we're talking buying properties for investment, exclusively.) You'll be shown the market, what houses are selling for at the current time.

This is also not to say that going out with an agent and looking but not finding isn't valuable. It is extremely valuable, because it quickly gets you up to speed on what houses are selling for. It informs you of the re-sale market at the time. And that, after all, is half the equation. You want to buy a home that you can turn around and resell at a profit. You can't do that until you know what houses are currently selling for.

Of course, the other side of the equation reveals itself when you find a house sufficiently lower in price than the market. *That's* where you make your profit.

Tip

You can sometimes get a good deal out of the current listings of properties by making "lowball" offers. You offer substantially lower than the seller is asking. If you have cash to loan, good credit, and can offer a quick sale, you can sometimes find a seller who must get out, has a lot of equity, and is willing to "give away" the house. (It's also a good deal for sellers, since without you there might be no sale and, possibly, fore-closure down the road.) Only don't count on it happening every time. My own batting average on this is closer to 10 or 11 to 1. (For every 10 or 11 lowball offers made, one gets accepted.)

Trap

The problem is that often agents don't like taking in lowball offers. It's hard work, and they hate the rejection that comes with being turned down. As a consequence, many agents simply aren't very good at getting a lowball offer accepted. If you're going to work with an agent, find one who's had a lot of success at lowballing.

Wait, Don't Leap

We'll look closer at where to find good deals in a few paragraphs, but first a word about timing. It's often the case (at least it is with me) that when the property is right, I don't have the cash. Or when I do have the cash and credit, the property isn't there. (It's a variation of the old theme, "Always a day late or a dollar short!")

Often properties at great prices become available when you aren't ready to buy. Maybe you're busy with some other project, or you have your capital tied up, or your personal life has some twists in it right then. You just can't be bothered. So you pass.

That's a mistake. Good deals in real estate are few and far between. Don't ever pass on a good deal. Even if the timing isn't right for you, make the time, borrow the money. If you have to, take in a partner.

Trap

The corollary is, don't buy a property just because *you're ready* to buy. Many people decide to purchase a rental property because they get a windfall of cash from an inheritance, bonus, or other source. Or they buy because a relative wants to sell and they want to help out. Or because they've decided they need to plan for their future retirement, and now is the time to get started.

Buying only because you're ready is often a mistake. The reason, simply put, is that just because you're ready to buy doesn't mean that there's a good deal out there waiting for you. Timing works both ways. Sometimes *you're* ready and the *market* isn't.

The only reason to buy a rental property should be because you have the opportunity to get it for a great deal. Never buy just because the time is ripe for you. The right price (and terms, etc.) makes for a good deal, not your personal timing.

Finding Those "Right" Properties

Having said that the important thing is to think in terms of selling before you buy, I'm sure you're wondering just where you find those wonderful properties that are so cheap. After all, if they're such a good deal, why hasn't someone else snapped them up?

Tip

Good deals are always available. They go to the ready, the quick, and the vigilant.

The truth is that there are always good deals out there. In order to find them you just have to immerse yourself in the real estate market around you, and I don't care where you are. Know enough people (brokers, lenders, escrow officers) in your area, and be known by them, and soon good deals will start to present themselves to you. Here are some of the ways that you can turn up good deals in your area.

1. Call the REO (Real Estate Owned) officers at several banks and savings and loans in your area. This person deals with foreclosed properties taken back by the lending institution. If you tell them the specific area and price range you are in, they may be willing to let you know of properties they are holding and would like to sell. Often these REOs are sold for close to market price, IF the lender carries the financing. If you pay cash (arrange for financing elsewhere), however, offer a quick sale, and take the property "as is," you can sometimes get a "steal." (Check Chapter 10 for more information on this subject.)

2. Check with four or five of the more active real estate offices in your area. Get to know the broker or the one or two agents who handle most of the investment properties. Let it be known that you're looking for good investment real estate.

When a good deal comes along, most agents and real estate offices would much rather make a commission in a quick sale than buy the property themselves, even if the price is severely depressed. After you get known, you'll get called. But be prepared to act immediately. You usually won't have much time to think it over. You'll be shown the deal and asked for an instant "yea" or "nay" answer.

3. Check the streets. Keep on the move yourself. Look at FSBO (For Sale By Owner) properties. Stop in, chat, and see if there's a deal in the making for you.

Also, check for vacant houses with weeds growing around that seem run-down and yet are in good neighborhoods. I have found more than one good deal this way. Perhaps an owner has moved out and is about to lose the property. Any offer will look mighty appealing to such a seller just then.

A quick check at the county recorder's office will tell you who owns the property. Call the owner and find out what the situation is. It could be a bankruptcy, foreclosure, or divorce, or on the other hand just careless owners. If it turns out that the property is about to be lost, make an offer. (This is a more technical realm and requires some additional expertise. I suggest you contact an attorney as well as check into my book, *Find Hidden Real Estate Bargains*, McGraw-Hill, revised 1991.)

4. Look for fixer-uppers. As the overall housing inventory in this country ages, more and more of these houses are becoming available. They can often be bought for a fraction of what their market cost would be if they were in great shape. Usually, however, they're in bad shape. They run the gamut from needing cosmetic repairs to requiring major reconstruction. Hence their low price.

Keep in mind with fixer-uppers, however, that the reason the price is low is that the property needs work, and that work will cost you money. Be sure that you factor in your costs of fixing-up before you buy. It may turn out that a house that seems very low-priced actually is too high, once the costs of getting it back into shape have been taken into account. If you're considering doing fixer-uppers, I suggest you check into *The Home Renovation Kit*, Dearborn Publishers, 1991, by my favorite author.

5. Attend auctions. These are being held with increasing frequency throughout the country. Sometimes real bargains can be had there. (See also Chapter 11 for more information.)

Calculating the Right Price to Offer

Finding the property is the first step. Deciding how much to offer is the next. Since the purchase price is critical to making a profit, offering too much may mean that you will lose money. Offering too little may mean that someone else will come in with a higher offer and you will lose out. The key, of course, is to find just the right price. But how do you do it? The answer is that you must work backward. Think of it as a mystery novel. In writing a mystery novel, the author always works backward. He or she first decides "who done it." Then the author works from back to front, dropping clues here and there until we get to the crime itself. (Of course, we as readers never see this "behind the curtain" work. We simply start at the beginning and work toward the end, marveling at the author's cleverness.) In terms of investment properties, the "who done it" is the resale and the "crime itself" is the purchase price. Just as in the mystery, to get to the beginning you have to work backward. Here's the procedure.

Step One. Identify the intended resale *price.* (The amount for which you figure you can resell the property.) As noted, you will be able to do this with increasing ease the more "for sale" properties you visit in your area. Eventually, you'll know just by driving by what a house should sell for.

Step Two. Estimate the costs of resale. This can include commission, attorney fees, escrow and title charges, and all other costs. Of course if you sell by yourself, you can avoid the biggest of these, the sales commission.

Tip

Figure that you will eventually resell for less than the going market price. If you price your home at only a few thousand less, you may find that you get an almost instantaneous sale. Also remember, buyers are extremely aware of price points (see the Introduction) in today's market. Get below that magic number, and you've got a sale.

Step Three. Estimate any costs of fixing up the property. These may be significant or minor, depending on the condition of the property you're considering. Check into *The Home Renovation Kit,* Dearborn Publishers, 1991, for estimating techniques.

Step Four. Estimate any costs of holding the property. These include such items as negative cashflow resulting from vacancy, maintenance, repair, etc.

Step Five. Estimate the costs of purchasing the property, exclusive of the amount of down payment.

Step Six. Add up steps two through five. Then subtract from step one. This is the maximum you can afford to pay for the property and break even. *You must pay less if you expect to make a profit.*

Example

Step One—Intended sales price		$150,000
Step Two—Costs of sale*	$3,500	
Step Three—Fix-up costs	2,500	

Step Four—Holding costs	1,500	
Step Five—Purchase costs	4,500	
	−12,000	−12,000
Step Six—Maximum purchase price to break even		138,000

*Sold "By Owner."

Trap

Don't raise the purchase price when you see how low it is. As you make this calculation in the real world, prepare to be shocked. On the surface it will immediately become clear that houses simply aren't selling for what you need to pay for them in order to make a profit. Rather, at first it will seem that all of them are selling for far more.

The tendency, therefore, is to adjust your figures upward. When they can't find what they want, many investors will go back and sharpen their pencils to come up with "adjusted" figures. They will reduce their estimated costs, and in so doing, up the maximum purchase price until it gets close to what the seller will take.

That's a mistake. Remember, you make your profit when you buy. Every dollar you increase the purchase price is a dollar you take away from profit. Increase the purchase price enough and the profit will be all gone, and you'll be into loss.

2

How to Successfully Invest in a Fluctuating Market

How can I justify buying a piece of property for investment today, when I can foresee that its value may go down significantly in the future?

This is the question that every investor asks when the market is fluctuating. The answer, of course, is to distinguish the valleys from the peaks.

It's impossible for me to know just what the market in your area is going to be like when you read this. It may be hot, lukewarm, stagnant, or falling. If it's any of the first three, chances are you'll know what to do on your own, in terms of investing. But if the market is falling, you could be throwing up your hands and saying, "There's nothing for me here!"

Not so. The greatest opportunities often occur in down markets. That's what this chapter is for. Here we're going to look exclusively at investing in real estate in hard times. (Note: We are going to be concerned at first with markets that are simply depressed. The prices may be falling, but there are still buyers. At the end of the chapter we'll consider a "blowout" market, when there is panic selling and virtually no buyers.)

A Depression Story

During the last *great* depression of the 1930s (as opposed to the rose-colored recession of the 1990s), a few very smart individuals made a huge amount of money in real estate. They made it during the depths of the depression, from 1933 to 1935. By the brief recovery of 1937, they were already wealthy. By the end of the Second World War, they were multi-millionaires. (And that was a time when a million dollars really was a lot of money.)

How they made it is a valuable lesson for those of us who are faced with trying to make money in the 1990s, when things also tend to be down.

Tip

Beware of false terms. No one I know of speaks of the 1990s as a "depression era." Yet, the similarities are unmistakable. Today we have more homeless people on our streets than at any time since the 1930s. We have had more bank and savings and loan failures. Counting those who have given up looking, we probably have more unemployed and underemployed than at any time since the 1930s. There are certainly more foreclosures than at any time since then.

All of which is to say, don't be fooled when economists call recent hard times a recession and not a depression. The only reason, in fact, that today may look different than the 1930s is because of all the safety nets in place now and not before—Social Security, bank insurers, Medicaid, unemployment compensation, etc. Pull away the veneer of normalcy they give, and the comparison to the 1930s is striking indeed.

Yet the 1990s may define a new kind of depression, one with a third of the country in it and the other two-thirds out. You should adjust your investment thinking accordingly.

Those who made money during the great depression made it by following a simple three-point plan.

First. They identified the bottom. The bottom, quite simply, is the place where the market stabilizes, below which prices won't fall further. Back in the 1930s the bottom was easier to define, since there was little modern financing (most property at the time had a mortgage value of fifty percent or less) and most sellers put down cash. Since almost no one would spend cash, property, especially housing, was essentially worthless. Until you wanted to buy it. Then the banks, who by then owned most salable property, wanted what they had into it, roughly 50 percent of the previous price. Thus, a kind of artificial bottom at that value was established.

Second. Once those old formidable investors had identified what banks would sell property for, they bought and then ruthlessly rented out the property, quickly evicting any unfortunates who couldn't pay rent.

They made enough to cover costs. And they made absolutely sure that the tenants paid. They were totally unforgiving of a tenant who wouldn't or couldn't come up with the money.

Third. At the first sign of a recovery, when prices turned up, they sold. Then when the recovery faltered, as it so often does, they went back and bought other properties, once again at bottom prices. They kept repeating the process, making profits along the way, until the real recovery came (which was the boom of the Second World War) and they saw their holdings explode in value into real fortunes.

Today's Market

Today's real estate market is different in significant ways from that of the 1930s. For one thing, prices are much higher and have remained higher, even through tough times. For another, the market has become more diversified. While real estate in one area of the country may be depressed, it could be flourishing in another. Yet another difference is that although thousands of lending institutions have failed, the federal government has bailed out the depositors, and thus confidence remains high in the banking system. As a result many more lending institutions remain solid, and there is a healthy supply of mortgages at low rates available to borrowers. Today, with strong credit and appropriate income, you can still buy a house with as little as five percent down.

Trap

Don't make the mistake of thinking that the real estate market around where you live is the same as it is elsewhere. During the late 1980s, for example, the housing markets in Texas and the midwest in general, as well as the northeast, were in a severe slump. At the same time, however, markets in New York, California and the rest of the west coast, and parts of the south were thriving.

On the other hand, into the mid-1990s as this is being written, almost the reverse has occurred. Markets in California, New York, and parts of the northeast have collapsed, while those in Texas and parts of the midwest are rallying.

During harsh economic times, the tendency is to want to "stay put." That could be a mistake. As noted, markets today are different in different areas. Sometimes it can pay big bucks to move. For example, a friend who had been having trouble finding work in California, where he was attempting to purchase a $200,000 home, recently moved to Illinois. There he found a good-paying job and purchased a home of comparable size for around $49,000, admittedly a bargain. He plans to live in it for a while, then sell it for a profit. His personal economic turnaround came about primarily because he understood that different parts of the country are in different phases of the economic malaise.

It's important to understand, however, that even in an area that is depressed, opportunities will exist. In fact, sometimes the greatest opportunities lie in areas where you can find a suitable full-time job and work on real estate investment on the side.

Buying in a Depressed Market

The key to buying successfully in a depressed market is to do what those savvy entrepreneurs in the great depression of the 1930s did, identify the bottom. Today, however, the bottom is more difficult to define. Today, mortgages are commonly given for about 80 percent of the sales price (although higher loan-to-value ratios are available). However, when prices fall it is often for much more than just 20 percent. In some areas of Texas, for example, prices between 1988 and 1991 fell by an average of about 30 percent. (This is based on sales prices, not asking prices.)

Thus, when owners found their equities wiped out, they frequently let the property go back to the bank. Yet when the bank tried to resell, it found that its mortgage was for more than the property was worth. During the 1930s, when banks found themselves in this situation, they could sometimes hold the property until times got better. Today, however, in part because of the sale of mortgages through the secondary markets and in part because of the fact that foreclosed property is accounted for as a debt rather than a asset, lenders can't simply hold. Lenders must quickly resell in order to keep paying interest on the money they owe to depositors. And they are doing so via auctions and silent broker sales (those in which the property is sold, without advertising, through a friendly broker to an investor) and other means as fast as they can. (See Chapter 10 for more details.)

Tip

Always consider foreclosed properties. Although lenders try to get top dollar, if you can offer a quick sale, cash, and an "as is" purchase, you can sometimes get a "steal."

Unfortunately, because lenders must resell foreclosed property quickly, they do not give support to a market bottom. Rather, by reselling foreclosures as fast as possible, they contribute to driving prices down. Add to this owners who find themselves in financial difficulty and are forced to sell for depressed prices, and you end up with a destabilized market.

It is very difficult today to determine what the bottom for prices in a depressed area will be when the market hasn't stabilized. How does a person who wants to invest in real estate in such an area, in fact, identify the true market bottom?

Wait Until It Stops Falling

This is the safest approach. The problem is, if you follow it, you could end up sitting on the sidelines for years. All the while, those who are willing to take a bit more risk, could be making money on the field.

Tip

You usually don't know where a market is until it's too late. By the time everyone agrees that real estate has turned up, all of the great buys will have long ago been sold.

Take a Chance

On the other hand, there are those who love the fact that the market is in terrible shape. For them, this only means that there are all kinds of opportunities. There are sellers who have to get out and will take ridiculously low prices for a quick sale. There are lenders overloaded with foreclosures who are dying to get rid of them and will dump them, often two and three at a time, again at very low prices for a quick sale. These entrepreneurs see an unstable market not as a threat but as an opportunity. They jump right in.

A Technique for Today's Market

In short, even if you can't identify the bottom or the point toward which the market may eventually fall, you should be able to tell where it is today. Knowing that and the fact that, given the hard economic times, you should also be able to pick up properties at significantly lower prices than the current market, you should be able to create a profitable margin, even in a market that might potentially fall further. The technique is simple:

Step One. Identify the current market. Don't worry where it will be a couple of years from now. Use the information on price points noted in an earlier chapter to help you here. The critical information, what you need to know, is what you can resell a home for, now. But, beware of a blown-out market (discussed later).

Step Two. Buy for significantly lower than the price point, the critical point at which the house can be resold. Search out the names of sellers who are desperate to dump their properties, either at banks disposing of REOs or at foreclosure sales.

Step Three. Resell. If you can offer a property that is still below the price point, still slightly below what people are willing to pay but high enough for you to make a profit, you've mastered the technique.

Tip

In the old days (prior to 1986), you really didn't want to buy and resell quickly, because to do so meant you couldn't take advantage of the capital gains taxes available to real estate. Since the passage of the 1986 tax reform act, however, the capital gains advantage for real estate has been almost erased. Thus, often you gain very little taxwise by holding for a longer period of time versus selling within a short time. (Always see your tax professional for tax advice.)

Comparison with a "Hot" Market

I often hear investors complain about a depressed market, saying such things as, "Nothing is selling." Or, "There simply aren't any opportunities."

Contrast this with a market that is sizzling hot, when prices are rapidly appreciating and there are two or three bids on every house that is offered for sale. Interestingly, in this "hot" market I also often hear statements such as, "Everything is so high-priced, there aren't any investment opportunities!"

The truth of the matter is that there are opportunities in almost every market. Surprisingly, they are roughly the same.

In a hot market the challenge is to find a house you can buy that doesn't have an inflated value. (Most sellers in such a market think their homes are worth far more than they are.) The challenge in a cold market is to find a house that is sufficiently low in price that it can be resold even in the tough times. (Sellers here tend to remember the former hot market and also often price their homes too high.)

Note that in both markets you are trying to do essentially the same thing: find a house that's inexpensive enough to purchase in order to offer a profit on resale. To my way of thinking, a down market sometimes offers an easier way to do this, since there are many more opportunities with distressed sales, auctions, foreclosures, etc. In a hot market you simply can't find the inexpensive properties.

Trap

Keep in mind that the other side of the coin is resale. In a hot market, resale is quick. In a depressed market it's slow, even with a good price. If you buy and need to resell *quickly* in a depressed market, no matter how good a deal you are offering you could end up losing.

Resale in a Blown-Out Market

In this book we are emphasizing that profit can be made not by renting out properties over time, but by reselling them fairly quickly. However, reselling in a depressed market, as noted, can be slow and sometimes painful.

A special problem occurs, however, when the market is more than just depressed. How do you resell when there has been a complete blowout in the real estate market, as has happened over the past five years in the northeast, Texas, Arizona, Southern California, and other areas? How do you resell an investment property you've bought when there's panic in the streets, when sellers will do *anything* to get out from under?

Tip

A market blowout is as much a psychological event as an economic one. During it, buyers behave much like a mob. Suddenly every buyer becomes convinced that the bottom has fallen out of real estate, and no one wants to buy. The psychological hang-up is that if you buy today and the price goes lower tomorrow, you will have lost money. Hence, don't buy today.

The result is that buyers hold back. It's not that there are no buyers out there. It's that they are afraid to jump into the market. They remain on the sidelines, and as a result the market falls further and faster. If you get caught in a blowout, try not to panic. Remember, there are buyers who will come back into the market, once the fear begins to dissipate.

In a blowout there simply aren't any buyers, and you won't be able to quickly resell your property. Hence, my advice is not to buy into this sort of market. Wait it out. Eventually prices will begin to stabilize, a bottom will start to form, and you can then begin to invest.

Trap

Another trouble with a blown-out market is that you can't really tell what constitutes a bargain. You may find a piece of property that you believe is being offered at half of its market value. You may purchase, only to discover that because buyers are afraid, you still can't resell even when you offer it at a very low price.

You can usually tell a market that's blown-out. For one thing, just read the newspapers. Reporters thrive on bad news, and the papers will be filled with reports of economic downturns and a falling real estate market. Interestingly, it's been my observation that each time a local paper comes out with a story explaining why the local housing market is in bad shape, sales tend to fall even further. It's the psychological effect we were noting earlier. Nothing breeds depression like news of it.

For a more precise determination of the market, you can ask a local broker for statistics on sales. Most belong to a co-broking service that keeps track of sales. When you see the number of sales year-to-year decline sharply for months in a row, you can pretty much assume the market has started to blow out. When sales grind to a virtual halt, you know you are in the worst of it.

You can also check with builders of new homes. New home sales, though not entirely in sync with resales, also reflect market conditions. In a blown-out market, new home sales will also be depressed. When builders are offering amazing deals, cutting prices, offering to help with financing, you can tell the market is pretty bad.

What to Do If You Get Caught in a Blown-Out Market

Obviously, what you want to do is to avoid buying into a blowout. The reason is two-fold. First, there's no telling how far or how fast the market will fall. Second, it's extremely difficult to resell any property, no matter how well priced (the psychological factor keeps potential buyers away).

Nevertheless, sometimes a depressed market will blow out unexpectedly. That's happened to me personally twice, once in Arizona and the second time in Southern California. (Note: The Southern California market is huge, and only portions of it actually went into free fall.)

If this happens you have two options. The first is to simply bail out at any cost, taking a loss, if necessary. The idea is that instead of devoting your energies and capital to what is essentially a losing proposition, you simply get out and move on. You can probably make more money in a different market in a shorter time than it would take you to recoup your investment in a blown-out market.

If you bought wisely, you should be able to sell at a distressed price and still not lose much money, if any at all, even in a blowout. True, not many houses are selling, but some always do sell, those with very low (bargain) prices.

The other alternative is to rent and hold (explored in the book of that name mentioned earlier). This works well only if you have a positive cashflow or at least not a negative one. (If you're into serious negative cashflow, then I strongly suggest you consider bailing out.)

Tip

Rental markets and sales markets often work in opposition. When the rental market is terrible, often home sales are flourishing. On the other hand when sales are depressed, the rental market is often strong. This means that in many cases it is possible to rent out a house that you cannot sell, and to hold for a long time.

Trap

Remember that in a blowout you are competing with sellers of homes who are giving them up to foreclosure. If you can't undercut their prices, you won't be able to resell.

Tip

When the market first falls in a blowout, it usually doesn't drop more than 20 percent, for a time. The reason is that sellers of homes typically have mortgages for 80 percent or more of their original purchase price. When prices drop below this 80 percent value, their equity is wiped out and they often allow the house to go into foreclosure, or issue the lender a "deed in lieu of foreclosure." Lenders then try to sell for their investment.

If you bought wisely, your purchase price should allow you to sell for less than this 20 percent artificial bottom, and if you plan to resell, you probably should do it as quickly as possible. The reason is that eventually lenders may find they can't sell their REOs and may lower their prices. Eventually they could lower them below the amount for which you can resell and still break even.

Bottom Line

Investing in a down market can be profitable, unless there's a blowout and the market collapses. It is riskier than an up market, because of the difficulty in reselling and the uncertainties that go with it. Nevertheless, I wouldn't stay away just because prices haven't entirely stabilized.

Tip

Remember, in a depressed market there are far fewer investors, hence the competition you will have is greatly reduced. In a hot market, investors are everywhere.

3
Prearrange All Financing

When you buy a home to live in, you have access to the best financing available. Further, you are generally interested in only a single mortgage, the one you get that allows you to make the purchase.

When you buy investment real estate, however, the financing is tougher, and you often may need additional financing after the purchase. For example, there may be repairs that need to be done before the property can be rented out or resold, or you may want to access some of your capital later on.

The point is that with an investment, it's not simply a matter of going out there and selecting from a vast array of mortgages that are available to you. It may be a matter of hunting just to find *any* mortgage. Further, once you get the mortgage, it's not always a matter of simply making the mortgage payments forever after. It may also be a matter of getting additional money.

Owner-Occupied Versus Investment

One of the biggest problems you'll face with investment property financing comes from the fact that you don't plan to occupy it. Lenders are far stricter in their financing with nonowner-occupied property. If you don't live in the property, you will probably find that you'll pay a higher interest rate, or more points, or be required to put up a bigger down payment, or all of the above. Further, when the real estate market in general is down, you may find that there are few, if any, lenders who will make any kind of loan for real estate investment.

Tip

The rule seems to be that when the market is rising, lenders are happy to loan money for investing in real estate. When the market turns down, however, the lenders close their doors to investors. Therefore, in down times, when there may be some real bargain prices out there, you'll have to be more creative in your approach to financing.

Owner-Occupied Financing

With owner-occupied property, you can get extraordinary financing. Today mortgages for up to 90 percent are readily available, and some lenders will even offer them up to 95 percent of the appraised value. You can get even higher financing if you qualify for a VA loan or are able to get an FHA loan. The key, however, is that you must occupy the property yourself.

This leads to an interesting consideration. What about actually living in the home? If you move in and occupy the property, you suddenly qualify for much better financing. I always encourage investors to try owner-occupancy whenever possible.

What this means, unfortunately, is that you tend to move around a lot. If you have a family with kids, you'll find this more difficult. On the other hand, moving every year or so to a different house can have it's up side. You'll get to live in a lot of interesting places.

Trap

Beware of claiming that you're going to move in to get the better financing, and then failing to make the move. Lenders are strictly regulated, and one of the strictest regulations has to do with owner-occupancy. It's one thing if you move in and live in the house for a year before deciding to rent it out. It's quite another to claim you'll move in, then immediately rent out the place. Doing the latter can get you in big trouble with the government regulators, and possibly result in your mortgage being called in.

Trap

Be sure to read your mortgage document carefully. Many mortgages given to owner-occupants prohibit the renting out of the property during the term of the mortgage. While I've never heard of this clause being enforced (indeed, it may not be possible for the lender to enforce it), it remains something to be aware of and concerned about.

Prearranging All Financing

Besides the difficulties in getting investment financing, there's also the matter of getting a big enough loan. Totally unanticipated problems often arise after a purchase that can make refinancing difficult if not impossible to obtain. Your own financial condition may change for the worse. The property may not qualify for additional loans. Lenders may be wary of lending you money so soon after you borrowed to purchase. For repairs, you may find that you can only get construction loans, which carry a higher interest rate and have many restrictions.

While you might indeed be able to get the financing you need after a purchase, you are running an unnecessary risk by not arranging it beforehand. And with real estate, there are risks aplenty without asking for more.

Trap

The biggest single financing mistake that new investors make is to assume they can get financing after they have made the purchase. Maybe they can, but maybe they can't. The time to get *all* financing, even if that just means arranging for financing that you may or may not want later on, is *before* you purchase.

Types of Financing Available

If you're going to buy property as an investment, there are a number of avenues to go down when it comes to financing. These generally include the following:

Institutional First (Including Draw-down)

Seller Assisted

Equity Line

While there are other methods of getting money out of a property, these are the most common options.

Institutional First (Including Draw-Down)

This is normally your first source. You could go to a bank, savings and loan, credit union, or mortgage broker. You would fill out an application, get a credit check, and so forth.

The problem would arise when you stated that you were intending to purchase for investment. Suddenly things would change. The biggest change would probably be in the loan-to-value (LTV) ratio.

As noted earlier, with owner-occupied property the LTV can be as high as 95 percent. With an investor, however, it's rarely over 80 percent.

Further, in a depressed or falling market, that ratio tends to drop. In 1992, for example, it was not uncommon to see some lenders drop the ratio to as low as 65 or even 60 percent. That means that to purchase, you'd need to come up with 35 to 40 percent down! (Plus, of course, qualify for the mortgage.) Needless to say, in difficult times an institutional first mortgage usually is not an investor's first choice.

The Draw-Down

Nevertheless, let's say that times aren't so tough, or that you do have a lot to put down. There is an advantage that an institutional first can offer, the "draw-down." Let's say you're buying a home that's basically a fixer-upper. You're getting it at a very low price, which is good. But after the purchase, you're going to have to spend a great deal of time and money restoring it to the point where it will be a good rental or a suitable resale. That could be bad. Let's further say that you've estimated it will cost you roughly $10,000 after the purchase to restore the property.

If you wait until after you have bought the property to go looking for a $10,000 loan, you could be in trouble. Refinancing a new first loan can be even tougher than getting one to make a purchase. Further, if the property is in run-down condition, lenders may balk at the idea of loaning you more money.

After the purchase, your only alternative may be a construction type of loan. Here you'll have to submit plans for the work to be done, and the money will be advanced to you only in stages, as you complete the work to the lender's satisfaction. Construction loans normally carry a higher interest rate than the new first mortgage you got when you purchased the property. The bottom line is that either you will pay more for financing after the purchase *or* you won't be able to get it at all. The better alternative is to arrange for financing before the purchase.

Which brings us back to that big new institutional first mortgage you may have gotten when you bought. (We're assuming here that you financed the purchase. If you were able to assume an existing loan the situation is different, as is the case with a seller financing the entire purchase.)

If you seek out a lender who will agree to give you the new first mortgage you use to purchase your property, you can also ask to receive the money in stages. The idea is to ask for more money than you would normally receive, the extra to be paid to you after the sale and after you've completed repairs.

Some lenders, particularly smaller banks, will give a much higher purchase money first mortgage, *if* you agree to do specific work on the property. Again, this is like a construction loan, but with a difference. Yes, you must submit plans and do the work, but the interest rate you are charged is not much higher than for the big first you secured.

For example, you may need a loan of $70,000 to buy the property and an additional $15,000 to fix it up. A lender may issue you an $85,000 first, with a draw-down. You get the first $70,000 upon purchase, and you get the balance as you complete the work you plan to do. Usually the interest rate and costs of this type of financing are significantly lower than going out and getting a construction loan separately for the $15,000.

Trap

Be sure you know *exactly* how much money you're going to need to fix up the property. Many new investors guess too low. Then, to their chagrin, once started they discover they can't finish on the money available. They have to go back to the lender for more.

Lenders don't like doing business with people who don't know what they're about. They especially don't like throwing good money after bad. If you go back to the lender and say, "Oops, I calculated wrong and need an additional $5,000," the lender is almost sure to say, "No way."

Seller-Assisted Financing

Of course, if you can't get an institutional first at a decent LTV with reasonable points and interest rate, you have to seek financing elsewhere. If the sellers are willing, you can have them carry the financing for you.

Seller-assisted financing can be the best you can get. What you do here is get the seller of the property to either lend you or outright give you the money you're going to need, either to fix up the property or to purchase or both. Let's first look at having the seller lend you the money.

Typical seller lending will look something like Figure 3-1.

You get a normal first mortgage, say for 70 percent of the purchase price. Then you get a seller-advanced second for 20 percent, and put 10 percent down. For a $100,000 property the deal looks like this:

$100,000 Property			
First Mortgage	=	$70,000	70%
Second Mortgage	=	20,000	20
Cash Down	=	10,000	10
Total		$100,000	100%

Typical Seller Lending

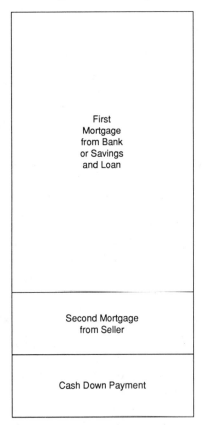

Figure 3-1 Sale involving seller financing (second mortgage).

Tip

The second mortgage given by the seller can be written almost any way both you and the seller agree. For example, the market rate for interest on a second may be 9 percent. But if agreed upon, you and the seller can set it at 7 percent.

A normal mortgage amortizes, that is, pays off monthly until it is entirely paid back. But you and the seller can agree to any term, including no payments for years until the mortgage is due back all at once. Thus, if you plan to resell, you can have no payments for, say, three years. Hopefully, by then you will have resold and paid off the second with interest. Along the way, however, you won't have been burdened with additional payments.

Seconds can be constructed in most creative ways, as long as the seller is willing to go along. And in recent times, with slow markets, most sellers have been increasingly cooperative.

Trap

All lenders use a ratio called "loan-to-value" when financing property. This LTV tells them the maximum mortgage they will offer. For example, if a lender's LTV is 80 percent, the maximum loan will be 80 percent of the appraised value.

Recently, however, lenders have been using a formula called "combined loan-to-value," or CLTV. This means that the maximum amount they will lend includes any secondary financing. For example, if you are buying a house for $100,000 and the seller is offering you a $10,000 second, this lender will only offer you a mortgage of $70,000.

Figuring CLTV		
Purchase price		$100,000
Combined loan-to-value 80%		
Maximum second	$10,000	
First	70,000	
Total		80,000
Required down payment		20,000

With a CLTV lender, the seller's second is subtracted from the first. Thus the amount you can borrow to purchase is limited. Be careful of CLTV lenders. Check them out before you get involved in borrowing.

Seller's Gift

Thus far we've been concerned with *borrowing* the money from the seller. But there is another and sometimes better avenue, getting the seller to give you the cash up front for free. If you are new to real estate the concepts here may be difficult to understand at first, so we'll go a step at a time.

Let's consider two different real estate transactions. In both we have a house whose investment value you have determined to be $100,000. In both cases, you estimate that it will cost you $5,000 to fix up the property.

In the first instance, you as a purchaser offer $95,000. You will pay your normal closing costs and the sellers will pay theirs, but you cut your price by $5,000 in order to compensate for the fix-up work you anticipate you'll have to do.

The sale progresses. The sellers clear title, you each pay your normal closing costs, and eventually you buy the property for $95,000.

The trouble is, you now need another $5,000 from somewhere to pay for the fix-up. Either you have to go out hunting for a construction loan, or you needed to prearrange a draw-down first, as noted earlier. In any event, somehow you have to come up with the extra cash.

There is a better way. In the second transaction, instead of offering the seller $95,000, you offer $100,000. However, you insist that the seller pay $5,000 of your closing costs. Thus, when the deal closes, your mortgage will be higher (80 percent of $100,000 instead of 80 percent of $95,000— a difference of about $4,000), your down payment will be slightly higher ($1,000 in this case), but you'll also have an additional $5,000 in your pocket that you didn't have to pay in closing costs. This can then be applied to the fix-up work you have in mind.

What you've actually done here is to finance part of the closing costs of the sale. You've increased the mortgage (and the down payment slightly), so that it covers part of the closing costs. That money saved is now yours to spend.

Note: In Figure 3-2 we have combined the seller paying for the buyer's nonrecurring closing costs with a second mortgage, thus significantly reducing the buyer's cash to get into the property.

Tip

The type of transaction noted above only works as long as the property will appraise for enough to cover the higher mortgage. Also, it has to be worded in such a way as to indicate clearly that you are indeed paying a higher price, as well as having the seller pay part of the buyer's closing costs.

Seller Pays for Closing Costs

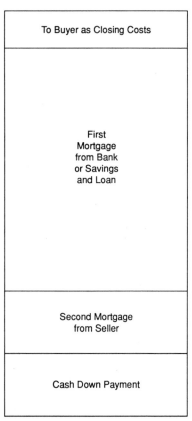

Figure 3-2 Financing part of the closing costs.

Trap

Lenders will normally allow the seller to pay for part of the buyer's closing costs as long as they are "nonrecurring." This term refers to such things as title insurance, attorney's fees, escrow charges, and even points. They will not, however, normally allow the seller to pay for buyer's interest payments, due at the time of closing.

In the past, lenders were far more lenient. Five years ago you could even write in that the seller could refund to the buyer part of the new mortgage, as much as desired! This was done in highly leveraged schemes where buyers purchased for nothing down and then actually received cash back!

Today lenders are quite strict, due to much stronger government regulation. No cash-backs are allowed on federally involved mortgages (virtually all institutional mortgages), and, as noted, the amount of allowance for closing costs is limited.

Equity Loans

This kind of financing for investors is a relative newcomer on the scene, yet provides some great options for getting money out of the property *after* you've made your purchase, if your property can qualify. It is typically called a "home equity loan," and was designed for people who own their home for a long time. Here, however, we're going to see how to get this loan even if you've just bought the investment property.

First, however, let's talk about refinancing in general after the purchase. Normally, institutional lenders won't let investors refinance a *first* mortgage for more than the amount currently owed on the property. For example if you owe $75,000, as an investor you might find a lender to loan you $75,000 on a first, plus the costs of refinance, but no more.

Why would you want to refinance in this case? The answer is that you might get a lower interest rate or otherwise better terms.

Tip

If you're *occupying* the property at the time you want to refinance, you can normally get up to 80 percent of the property's current value (higher in some cases) on a new *first* mortgage, regardless of whether that means you'll be pocketing money in addition to paying off old financing. It's something to keep in mind when refinancing to get profits out.

The alternative is a home equity loan, which is basically a *second* mortgage. (Mortgages are listed in the order on which they are placed on the property. The lower the number, the greater the security for the lender.) Home equity mortgages were originally only available to those who wanted to borrow on owner-occupied property. Over the last few years, however, they have become available to owners of income property as well. Today, an equity loan with investment property as collateral, when available, typically will carry a less than 1 percent higher interest rate (than owner-occupied) and the costs for getting it will be virtually identical as for owner-occupied.

Except in really depressed markets, these loans are available from most banks and savings and loans. The key to them is equity. They are based on your equity in the property. The greater your equity, the greater the loan. Typically they involve a maximum of 75 to 80 percent CLTV (combined loan-to-value). For example, if you have a property worth $100,000 and have a $60,000 existing first mortgage, you probably can borrow an additional $15,000 to $20,000 with this type of loan.

Your purpose in getting this loan can be anything. You may want to use the money to fix up the property or simply to withdraw your capital. The lender really doesn't care, as long as the equity is there.

The Problem with Recent Purchases

This raises a problem for an investor who has recently bought a piece of property. Let's say that you bought with 20 percent down and an 80 percent new mortgage. Now you want to get an equity loan. However, because these loans typically will not be higher than 80 percent and because you already have a loan for 80 percent, presumably you can't get one.

Not so fast. It all depends on the appraisal. You may have bought your house based on an appraisal of $100,000 on July 1. However, if on August 1 a new appraiser for an equity lender says it's worth $120,000, you can now qualify for an equity mortgage of $16,000. Here's how it works:

Purchase price	$100,000	New Appraisal	$120,000
80% mortgage	80,000	New 80% Mort.	96,000

The key, of course, is getting that new appraisal for a higher amount. How can you get an appraisal for $120,000 a month after you've purchased a property for $100,000? It would seem that your purchase price established the value of your property, at least for a period of time probably extending six months into the future. Unless property values have soared overnight, how could an appraiser justify such an increase?

Rest assured, it *can* be done. I secured such financing myself just a few months ago. It wasn't hard, and it wasn't illegal. Remember, it's all based on *equity*.

Judging Your True Equity

While a sale does establish the market price for a home, it's important to understand that appraisers do not rely simply on one sale, even if it's the house in question. Rather, they check out as many as four or five sales of comparable houses in the area.

Let's say that houses in the area have sold for around $125,000. However, sales were slow and you found a desperate seller. Perhaps the yard was a mess and the house desperately needed repainting. It simply looked so bad that it wouldn't sell.

So you offered and bought for $100,000. Then you spent a couple of hundred dollars and a few weekends cleaning up and landscaping the yard, and repainting the front and some of the interior of the house. Then you went to a new lender (not the one that loaned you the purchase money for the first mortgage) and asked for an equity loan. You explained you got a "steal" because the house was in terrible condition. But now you've fixed it up and you want a new loan, which, based on comparables, you determine to be $125,000. (When you apply for an equity loan, you will typically ask for a specific loan amount.)

A different appraiser comes out and checks the comparables. Then the appraiser checks your house. (For equity loans the appraiser often doesn't even come inside, but instead "drives by," taking a picture of the property.)

There is every likelihood that you'll get a higher appraisal. It doesn't really matter what you paid, as long you can justify a higher price now (after the cosmetic work you did). The only thing that really does matter is that you have sufficient equity to justify the loan.

One thing to remember, however, is that you want to be sure you get a lender who handles investment equity loans. As I noted, these may end up costing slightly more in interest, but other than that are about the same as for owner-occupied. Be aware, however, that not all lenders offer these.

Trap

There are two types of home equity loans. The first is a fixed-amount loan. You borrow, for example, $10,000, and the lender writes out a check for that amount to you.

The second type is a revolving loan in which you can take out any amount up to the maximum and repay at any time, with the loan remaining in force. It's sort of like a Visa or Mastercard loan. The revolving type of loan is usually best for an investor, since it gives you maximum flexibility.

Tip

There are "equity lenders" who will offer mortgages, typically of 65 percent or less, based exclusively on your equity in the property *without qualifying*. They don't care if you have terrible credit, and no income with which to repay. (In fact, sometimes they are hoping you can't re-pay so they can foreclose and get the property!) They charge a much higher interest rate, perhaps 5 percent higher, and more in points and other fees. Be careful of these lenders, unless you have a plan to quickly resell and get out.

4

How to Accurately Estimate Operating Costs

If there's an Achilles' heel for most investors, it's the ability to accurately predetermine the costs of operating a real estate investment. Most investors can calculate to the penny how much it's going to cost them to get in. Many can come pretty close to figuring how much it will cost them to resell. But when it comes time to estimate how much it will cost in between purchase and sale, most are way off.

Note: When we talk about "operating costs" in this chapter, we are not talking about mortgage principal and interest payments, taxes, and insurance. Those are costs involved in virtually any property ownership. Here we're concerned with costs such as maintenance and repair that are over and above "PITI."

Guessing wrong about operating costs can be a serious problem, and can mean the difference between making a profit and losing money. This is particularly the case when you're investing in a house where the margin for error is small. For example, if you figure that your costs over and above income will be only $1,000 over a year, and they actually turn out to be $10,000, chances are your profits are out the window and you've got a serious loss to worry about.

Why It's Hard to Estimate Actual Costs

The operating costs of any real estate investment tend to have enormous variables. Even when you're dealing exclusively with houses, one property may cost twice as much as another to operate over a year. Until you've actually purchased the property, it's difficult to know what those costs will be. Here are some of the variables that can adversely and unexpectedly affect operating costs of any real estate investment:

Unexpected vacancies

Repairs

Government interference

Increased maintenance

Utility problems

We'll look into how to predict possible operating costs before you purchase later in the chapter. But for now, let's consider some of the unexpected costs of owning investment real estate that you could run into.

Unexpected Vacancies

When most people buy a real estate investment, such as a rental house, they add in a vacancy figure of 5 percent. Why 5 percent? I suppose simply because it's what's been done for years. Yet the figure is arbitrary and, in my experience, usually way off.

Tip

Some months of the year are easier to rent homes than others. Usually the easiest months to rent are July and August, the reason being that people want to get in and settled before school starts. Most don't like to move during the school year.

On the other hand, the hardest months to rent are December and January. People don't like to move during the winter, and particularly around the holidays.

Your vacancy factor depends to a large measure on when your last tenants move out or when you first "rent up". As noted, for example, if you purchase in October or November, it's not inconceivable that you will have to wait several months to rent up your home, simply because of the time of year. On the other hand, if you buy in May or June, you may find that it's easy to rent almost immediately. If you rent immediately and the tenant stays in for the full year, you have a zero-percent vacancy factor that year. If you can't rent for two months, your vacancy factor for that year is 17 percent.

Trap

Beware of tenants who want leases that expire around the end of the year. It may suit the tenant's needs very well, but it could mean you'll have to wait longer to rerent. If possible, shorten or lengthen leases so that they expire during the summer months.

In addition to normal vacancies, there's also the matter of tenants who won't pay and/or won't move. While precautions can be taken here, such as careful screening, you can never know when a tenant will turn out to be a "bad apple."

I have gone years in renting property and not had a single tenant who was more than a week or so late in rent. And at other times I've had two or even three properties nonperforming, because tenants couldn't or wouldn't pay their rents.

The truth is that tenant problems are completely unpredictable. You can't really anticipate them in most cases, and you can't really set aside a percentage of income to deal with them when you're a small investor.

Trap

One of the problems of owning only one investment property is that when your tenant doesn't pay, you suddenly have a 100 percent rental problem. (If you owned 20 properties and one didn't pay, you'd have only a 5 percent problem.) That's another reason not to stick with a set percentage number when you calculate your operating costs due to vacancies and evictions.

Tip

There are many predictors of tenant behavior that landlords use when renting, so as to avoid getting a tenant who won't pay and/or won't leave. These include checking credit, checking bank accounts, and verifying employment. But the most reliable predictor I have found is to call the tenant's previous landlord, *once removed*. Once removed means not the current landlord (who may say anything just to get rid the tenant), but the landlord before the present one who has nothing to lose by telling you if the tenant was good or bad. If a tenant can't or won't supply the name of the once-removed landlord, I won't accept that tenant.

If you get a tenant who won't quit or pay, you not only have the cost of lost rent, but you also have the cost of eviction. Eviction in most states is relatively swift, typically three to six weeks. But today it almost universally requires going to court via an Unlawful Detainer Action. That means an attorney, unless you've done it enough times to act as your own lawyer, plus some court fees, plus other possible costs.

By the time you get through with an eviction proceeding it may have cost you several months' rent plus twice that amount in legal fees. Again, because this is hopefully a rare occurrence, most investors don't count on it happening and don't figure it into the operating cost equation when they buy a property. It's another unpredictable variable. However, if you invest on a regular basis you have to assume that sooner or later, you will need to evict a tenant.

Tip

You may be able to cut costs by negotiating first.

The worst thing you can do with a balky tenant who won't pay, in my opinion, is to stay aloof. Talk to the tenant (assuming they're willing to talk). Find out what the problem is. In most cases it's a matter of a change in circumstances, such as a job loss or illness or other extenuating circumstance that prevents the tenant from being able to make payments. Chances are the tenant knows that eviction is a possibility and wants to move, but financially can't.

Quietly, but firmly, you can point out that an eviction can be reported to credit reporting agencies and that bad credit will be the result. Further, most tenants have some resources such as savings accounts that they don't want to touch unless it's an emergency. (It's surprising how many tenants don't see the inability to pay rent as an emergency!) You can suggest that they use these funds.

Finally, if all else fails and they want to move but don't have the funds, you may offer to pay for their move (the money to be paid only upon their leaving, of course). Yes, it's your money gone, but if it gets them out sooner and saves you eviction costs, you may save money in the end.

Trap

Be aware that evictions don't always run smoothly. A tenant may contest an eviction in court. Although it happens rarely, this could delay eviction by weeks or even months. If there is an illness or a bankruptcy involved, the delay could be longer.

Unexpected Repairs

Another unexpected cost of operation that may not be taken into account when making a purchase is that of repairs to the property. Much of this can be covered by careful examination of the property prior to purchase, but not all. This is particularly the case when you have owned the property for more than a year.

Tip

When you purchase, be sure to get a written disclosure statement from the seller (now required in California, and soon to be required in most other states) describing all defects in the property. Later, if you discover a long-standing defect that wasn't listed, you may be able to force the seller to pay for repairs.

Trap

Generally speaking, the longer you own the property, the harder it is to go back to the seller to force payment for repair work. After a year, except in unusual circumstances, getting the seller to pay will be extremely difficult.

A seller's disclosure statement can protect you from some undisclosed repair problems. A termite clearance, required for most mortgages, can protect you as well. For example, recently a friend purchased an investment home and received a termite clearance on it.

As soon as it had been rented up, the tenants called and in frightened voices explained that their refrigerator had fallen through the floor and into the basement. It turned out that termites had eaten away the flooring beneath the refrigerator. The termite company that issued the clearance paid for the repair of the flooring, a new refrigerator for the tenants, and all work required to get the termites out.

On the other hand, another friend recently bought an investment house and the seller disclosed that the roof was old, but not currently leaking. During the first really bad winter rain, however, winds blew off shingles that were badly worn and rain came in. Repair proved impossible, and a new, and expensive, roof was needed.

The sellers refused to pay for a new roof, however, arguing that when

they had lived in the property, it hadn't leaked. Indeed, the leaks occurred only when winds blew off some shingles.

The investor's insurance company paid for the blown-off shingles,
but the investor had to pay for a new roof. A costly and unexpected operating expense.

Tip

You can anticipate many repair costs before you buy by getting a thorough home inspection. A good inspector can inform you of those items
that are likely to go out, such as a worn roof, an old and battered water
heater, bad electrical circuits, leaking plumbing, a worn-out heating
system, etc. See Chapter 7 for more details.

Trap

Beware of inexperienced or incompetent inspectors. State licensing of
home inspectors is in its infancy, and many current inspectors are simply contractors or even construction laborers who have bought some
fancy cards and taken out an ad. If the inspector you hire doesn't know
any more than you do, not only is your money wasted but you could be
setting yourself up for expensive trouble later on down the road.

There is a national association of home inspectors, ASHI (American
Society of Home Inspectors), and it's a good idea to ask if your inspector belongs. But even better is a recommendation from local real estate
agents. Often agents use two or three inspectors whom they can recommend as reliable. I have found these recommendations to be valuable,
since the agents themselves are at some risk if an inspection is bad,
hence they are on the lookout for good ones.

Ultimately, of course, a home system can break down unexpectedly
even in spite of thorough inspections. To avoid this, my suggestion, as
noted earlier, is to stick with newer houses. Your chances of having repair problems greatly increase with the age of the property.

Costs of Government
Interference

This is a relatively new problem with real estate ownership, and one
with which most investors are, as yet, unfamiliar. Yet it is becoming increasingly onerous, and can lead to unexpected operating expenses.

The example that comes to mind is that of a lovely city in Southern

California that has a preponderance of spacious rental homes. A few landlords, in order to get higher rents, had taken to renting their single-family properties to more than one family. As a result there was increased noise, more cars on the street, and in general more people in the properties than there should have been. Of course, neighbors complained.

The city fathers, who already had ordinances to control noise and excessive car-parking, decided in their wisdom to instead restrict the right of property owners to rent. They imposed a ban on having more than four adults in any single-family property. (An adult being anyone 18 years of age or older.)

This meant that if you had an investment house and you wanted to rent to a couple who happened to have three children living at home over the age of 18, you could not do so, unless you made a special appeal to the city. (It's interesting that owner-occupants of property could have as many adults as they wanted living on the premises.)

The result of this local ordinance was to impose a harsh (and in my opinion unjustified) restriction on the investor's ability to rent. It just might mean that you'd have to reject an ideal tenant. (The ordinance is being challenged in court.)

Other restrictions that are sometimes imposed by local governments include rent control (usually on properties of four or more units) and licensing and fees on investors who rent property. There may be other governmental restrictions imposed in your area.

All of these ordinances and other forms of government interference usually translate into higher costs for you. It may be in the form of longer vacancy periods while waiting for a tenant who fits the city's profile, or direct costs in the form of taxation, or even limitations on the amount you can charge for rent.

Tip

It's a good idea to investigate these sorts of potential operating costs before you buy. Check with property managers in your area. They are the people who are usually most up-to-date on such matters.

Increased Maintenance Costs

Maintenance is the most underrated cost of operating a rental property. Most investors simply ignore it when they are calculating their costs prior to making a purchase. "Oh yes, there'll be some maintenance," they say to themselves, and then promptly dismiss it. That's a mistake.

All properties have maintenance costs. (These are separate from repairs. Repairs happen when something breaks, such as a water heater, and must be replaced. Maintenance means keeping the place up even when nothing is broken, as in the case of gardening or pool service.)

There are two kinds of maintenance costs. One is monthly, or ongoing. The other is periodic, and occurs only when there is a vacancy and a need to rent up the property.

Ongoing Maintenance

Ongoing maintenance costs typically include the following:

Pool service

Lawn and garden service

Pest control

Garbage collection

Many investors assume that once they become a landlord, the tenant will pay for the above services. Indeed, the lease may call for the tenant to pay for them. That, however, could be a mistake.

Tip

Most tenants won't pay for anything that doesn't directly benefit them. For example, they will pay for garbage pickup in most cases. But they won't pay for ongoing pest control unless they are bothered by bugs right at the moment. Even if you require them to pay for such services by lease, they may refuse to do so.

Trap

Don't have tenants take care of pools. In all the years I've rented, I've never had a tenant who could adequately take care of a pool. Tenants may have good intentions, but usually they are untrained. If they are expected to pay for chemicals, they may tend to skimp on them. Pools need to be cleaned weekly, and tenants may not find the time. Over the course of several months, the condition of the pool can deteriorate badly. The result can be a damaged pool motor or filter or, what's worse, damaged plaster, which could require the pool to be drained and either cleaned or repaired.

When dealing with lawn and garden, a lot depends on how good you want your house to look. I've found that if I plan to resell soon, I want the house to look sharp, at least from the front. Yet it takes a long time to get a lawn growing well and to have shrubs full and green. If I leave this work to a tenant, my experience is that only the minimum gets done. Yes, the lawn may be mowed, and the shrubs trimmed occasionally. But weeds will appear, and little to no fertilizer will be used. The only way to ensure that the lawn and garden look good is to have it done professionally, and to pay for it yourself.

Adding Costs to Rent

As a result of the fact that tenants probably won't care for your house the way they would for their own, many landlords will agree in a lease to pay for a gardener, for pool service, for pest control, and, in an apartment situation, even for garbage collection. The costs for all these services, however, can be quite high, as much as several hundred dollars a month. This can make a real dent in the cashflow of the property and throw it into a negative cashflow situation. If you were to buy not anticipating these sorts of ongoing maintenance costs, they would come as a very rude shock.

Once faced with large ongoing maintenance costs, some landlords ask a higher rent, pointing out to tenants that gardening, pool service, etc. is included. My experience is that you are able to retrieve only a portion of the costs in this manner. For example, if a gardener and a pool service cost a total of $150 a month, you can probably increase rents by $75 and still keep the property fully rented. But if you increase rent by the actual costs, most tenants will opt for a competing property where rents are lower and they are expected to handle some of the services.

In short, while you can recoup some of your costs here, chances are you won't be able to recoup them all.

Utility Costs

Finally, there's the matter of ongoing utility costs. These usually include:

Water

Gas

Electric

Phone

Water

Most investors who own single-family residences opt to pay only for water. They pay for water because if they don't, the tenant may not water the yard and garden enough and plants and lawn will die.

In my experience, when the tenants are paying the water bill, they tend to assume that everything growing in your yard is drought-resistant. And in order not to run up their bills, they may keep watering to a minimum. Therefore, if you want your yard to look lush and green, in most cases you'll need to pay for the water.

Trap

If you pay for the water, the tenants may use it lavishly, sometimes overwatering. I have seen tenants leave sprinklers on for days, not caring because they weren't paying for it.

Tip

You can write into your rental agreement a clause stating that you'll pay for a certain maximum amount toward water. Any use over that amount and the tenant will be responsible for it. This is a compromise that sometimes works.

In those areas of the country that are in true drought conditions (such as the west in recent years), the water problem can be even more ominous. Water rationing can produce some astonishingly high water bills. (Typically, in a rationing situation, the utility company allows for a small amount of water at the normal cost, then adds penalties for overuse.)

I once had a tenant who, fortunately, was paying for his own water. His first water bill was for over a thousand dollars! He screamed and fussed, but it turned out he had immensely overused water in a rationing situation. He refused to pay, and eventually the utility turned off his water and he moved out. Fortunately, I was not responsible for his water bill. But I did have to find a new tenant.

Trap

In rationing situations, if you insist that the tenant pay for the water, the result is often dead lawns and shrubs. If you plan to resell and want the yard looking good, you'll probably have to "bite the bullet" and pay the water costs yourself.

___

Buyers don't buy properties with dead lawns and shrubs. Even if it's in a drought situation, the buyers always expect the lawns to be green and the shrubs to be full and lush. You could lose a sale, or get a significantly lower price, if you allow the yard and garden to die while trying to save on watering costs.

Gas and Electric

Gas and electric are normally paid by tenants. However, be wary if you buy a multiple-unit building. Sometimes there aren't separate gas and electric meters. When that's the case, you may be forced to pay for these utilities yourself. That could be quite an unexpected maintenance cost.

Phone

A resort situation is the only one I can think of where a landlord/investor would pay for a phone. I once had a property near a lake that was rented out weekly. I paid for all utilities, including phone. Of course I was getting a very high rental rate, so that made it worthwhile.

___

If you're paying for phone, check with your local phone company to see if they can install a "local-call-out-only" feature. This feature prevents the tenant from using your phone to dial outside a specific geographical area or outside a specific area code. Some phone companies that do not have this service will provide an "incoming only" phone service, but that is not nearly as desirable, for the tenant almost certainly will want to call out, particularly in an emergency.

Calculating Operating Expenses Before Purchasing

We've covered the various operational expenses that are often ignored, overlooked, or discounted when an investor prepares to purchase a property, including:

Unexpected vacancies

Repairs

Government interference

Increased maintenance

Utility problems

On the other hand, as we've seen, if these are fully taken into account, and the investor sets aside reserves or agrees to pay for them on a monthly basis, they could absorb virtually all of the cashflow from some properties. So what are you to do when you are considering the purchase of a property? Account for all the possible operational costs and then find you can't afford any property? Or ignore them and end up losing money?

My suggestion is a compromise that involves the use of a time line. (Too few investors use this technique, and, unfortunately, either miss good deals or get into bad ones.)

Time Line Planning

A time line simply is a plan for the entire ownership of a piece of property. Let's say you find a wonderful investment house. The price is right, and you figure you can resell soon for a good profit. Before making the purchase, I suggest you create a time line that looks something like the following:

Time Line for Operating Costs									
	*Jan.	Feb.	Mar.	Apr.	May	Jun.	Jul.	Aug.	Etc.
Vacancy									
Repairs									
Government									
Maintenance									
Utilities									

*Fill in the months you anticipate owning the property, whether it be for just a few or *for several years.*

The entire purpose of the time line is to allow you the opportunity to plot possible operational costs during your time of ownership. If you're careful and do it conscientiously, you can begin to see what your likely costs will be. More importantly, you can see *when* they will occur.

Sometimes what you'll discover is that if you hold the property for, say, five years, you'll end up paying an enormous amount, particularly in terms of repairs and potential vacancies. On the other hand if you hold it for only one year, you may find that you can avoid those problems—resell before they occur.

Similarly with maintenance, you may find that if you hold the property during the winter months, your costs for water, for example, may be nil because of rains. On the other hand if you hold in summer, in a drought situation, your water costs to keep the place green and looking attractive for resale could be staggering.

Tip

In a drought situation, for a short-term investment, it's best to buy in the fall and sell in the spring. That way you avoid the harsh summer months and take advantage of the wetter winter months.

Creating a time line doesn't mean that certain operational costs aren't going to exist. Rather, it gives you the opportunity to see when they will occur and to plan your ownership accordingly. For example, if you can turn the property over very quickly, you may never need to rent it out! You can calculate and absorb several months of mortgage, taxes, and insurance in your purchase plan, figuring you'll save on advertising and cleanup and have the place ready for new buyers.

The Bottom Line

You are going to have some operational costs whenever you purchase an investment piece of real estate. These costs can sometimes be very high, at other times only moderate. The key to success in investing, however, is knowledge, and in this case knowledge of when and how much these costs will be. If you know what they are and plan for them *before* purchasing, chances are you'll have a successful investment. Nothing hurts worse than to buy a property figuring you'll have a margin of $xxx that will be your positive cashflow, only to find it's been wiped out by unexpected operating costs.

5

Converting Your Current Home to a Rental

There are currently over 60 million homeowners in America. And statistics suggest that the average homeowner moves about every seven to nine years.

If you already own a home and are thinking about moving, why not think a little deeper and consider converting your present home (the one you would otherwise sell) into a rental? It's a cheap, effective, and easy way to get into real estate investing. And since you already own your home, you're halfway there!

The Strategy

Before we get into the nuts and bolts of how to make it work, let's take a moment to be sure we're clear on what's involved. Here we're talking about taking your current home, the one in which you live and on which you make mortgage payments, and renting it out to someone else.

Obviously this works only if you're no longer living there. (We're not here considering taking in roomers—that's a different subject.) What it means is that you will move someplace else, perhaps a different part of town or even out of the city.

Usually this strategy works only for someone who is considering a move anyhow. Perhaps you are changing jobs and must move. Or maybe your home is just too small for your family and you want to move to a bigger house. Or perhaps you've come into some money and are now able to step up to a better neighborhood. The reason for the move is irrelevant. What's important is that you've decided to move no matter what.

Normally, what you would do is to sell your current home and use the money to buy a new home. You'd start with one house and end with one. Here, however, we're considering buying a second house while still keeping your first one. You start with one house and end with two.

This strategy is the one that countless people have used to make their first true investment in real estate. It's worked in the past and it continues to work today, as long as you watch out for the pitfalls.

Getting Your Money Out

The biggest and most immediate problem with converting your present home to a rental is getting enough money out to purchase a new home for yourself. However, if you go about this correctly, it's usually not as hard as it may first seem.

The key is to borrow enough money on your current home to make a down payment on a new home. That way you get to keep your current property as well as purchase a new one. For example, let's say that you have lived in your current home for eight years and you have $55,000 of equity.

Mortgage	$75,000
Equity	55,000
Market Value	130,000

Normally you would sell the property. Let's say you pay 10 percent in costs (real estate commission, escrow charges, title insurance, etc.) That's $13,000 off the top. If you get a cash buyer and don't have to take back any paper, you end up with around $42,000 net to invest in a new home.

On the other hand, let's say that you keep the old property and refinance to get some cash out. You increase your mortgage(s) to 80 percent of value, or $108,000, and you pocket roughly $30,000 (there are always the costs of refinancing). You still own your present home. But you now take this $30,000 and invest it in a new one. Of course, $30,000 isn't as much as $42,000 for a down payment on a new house, but it's probably enough. And the advantage is you get to keep your old home.

You now move into your new home and then rent out your old one.

Hopefully the rental income will cover your old house's mortgage costs plus at least taxes and insurance. Your old home now becomes an investment property and, depending on your income level, you may be able to deduct not only your actual expenses but depreciation, too. (See Chapter 12.)

Benefits of Conversion

The benefits, thus, are the following:

- You keep your old house and, hopefully, get appreciation as its value goes up.
- You possibly get a decent tax write-off from your old property.
- You get a new house and the ability to write off taxes and mortgage payments on it.

Even in today's up-and-down real estate market, I have seen couples convert their current home into a rental and thereby gain significant tax savings plus equity appreciation, even in the first year.

Trap

You should be aware that if your gross adjustable income exceeds $100,000 you will not be able to write off all or perhaps any of the taxable loss on your investment property. There are strict guidelines to follow. Check with your accountant or tax planner.

Further, depending on your tax situation, there could be undesirable tax consequences by refinancing. At the least, if you sell later on you may find that you receive less cash (because you borrowed on your equity earlier on) and yet you still have to pay taxes on a large gain. Check with your accountant or attorney for details here.

Plan Ahead

It's important to understand that when you are planning to convert your present home to a rental and then buy a new house, timing is very important. For one thing, you must arrange for all your financing *before* you begin to look for your new house.

The reason for working far ahead is that most lenders won't accept money for a down payment that's been borrowed. Therefore, you must get your money out early and let it "age" for a while in the bank.

Tip

___

Most lenders figure that if you've had the money for a down payment in your bank account for three to six months, it's your reserve and can be used as a down payment. However, if you borrow money and then immediately use it to buy, they assume you borrowed specifically to purchase, which is a no-no. This makes a kind of weird sense, in that if you can afford to keep the money in the bank for a while, make your regular house payments, and maintain a good credit rating, you probably *are* capable of handling a new house and new mortgage.

Homeowner Advantages When Refinancing Your Existing Home

Generally speaking, as a homeowner who is occupying a property, you can get the very best real estate refinancing available. For example, if you were an investor with a rental property and you wanted to refinance, most institutional lenders (banks, savings and loans, etc.) would restrict the amount you could borrow to the existing financing plus costs. (See Chapter 3 on financing.) In our example given above, you could borrow only the amount of the mortgage ($75,000 in this case) plus the costs of refinance. Not much help here. To get additional financing, you'd need to get a second mortgage, home equity mortgage, or something of the kind, usually at a higher interest rate than a first mortgage.

As an owner/occupant, however, you can refinance for up to 80 percent (sometimes as much as 90 percent) of the market value of your property, regardless of the current financing on it. Thus you could indeed, in our above example, borrow enough money for a down payment on another property through the use of a new low-interest first mortgage.

Trap

___

Lenders require that you state your plan to occupy the property on which you are borrowing. Be sure that you don't move out as soon as you get the financing. Also, some lenders require that you sign a statement saying you will not rent out your home once you get the mortgage. While this kind of a clause is probably not enforceable, you don't want to be arguing legalities with a large lender. Best get a lender who doesn't have such a clause in the mortgage.

Tip

Given the fact that as a homeowner/occupant you can borrow up to 80 or 90 percent of current value, the tendency for most owners is to go for the maximum amount. This could be a mistake.

Remember, the strategy for borrowing on your current home in order to buy another only works if you can rent out your old house for enough money to pay for your basic expenses (mortgage payments, taxes, and insurance). If it turns out that borrowing the maximum saddles you with payments of $1,500 a month and you can rent the property for a maximum of only $1,000 a month, it will cost you $500 a month for basic expenses. When you incur maintenance and repairs on top of that, you'll feel overwhelmed and regret the day you kept the property.

Trap

Don't overborrow. If the house can't be rented for enough to make the payments on a loan, you could find it a drain on your regular income to the point where you might even lose it to foreclosure. Figure out in advance your costs, and then base the maximum amount you can borrow on payments that can meet those costs.

If you can't borrow enough at payments low enough to be met by rental income, your house isn't a suitable candidate for a rental. You may be better off simply selling and buying another property.

What to Consider Before Beginning

If you think you might indeed want to borrow on your present home for a down payment on a new one, and then keep the existing house as a rental, there are a number of questions you first need to answer. These include the following:

- Will increasing my debt on the old property decrease my chances of qualifying for a new loan on the new property?
- Are current mortgage market conditions (interest rates) favorable for a conversion?
- For how much can I reasonably expect to rent my old house?
- Is my old house suitable to be a rental property?
- What is the rental market like in my area?

- How will I handle management of the property once it becomes a rental?

We'll spend the rest of the chapter answering these important questions.

Changing Your Debt Ratio

When you buy a new house, chances are you're going to need to qualify for a new loan. (There are exceptions. You could pay cash. Or you could find an assumable loan. However, for now we're going to assume you do the standard sort of thing and get a new loan.)

In order to qualify for a new loan, a lender looks at three things:

1. Your cash reserves, to see if you can afford the down payment.

2. Your credit, to see that in the past you have repaid loans that you have borrowed.

3. Your income, to see if you can afford to make the monthly payments.

When you refinance your old house you increase your cash reserves and, presumably, you don't change your credit history. However, you may adversely affect the income you have available to use to qualify for a new loan. Let's consider an example.

Helen and Peter decide to refinance their old home in order to purchase a new one. Their old monthly payments (taxes, insurance, and mortgage) came to $500 a month. However, after refinancing, they figure their new payment will be $1,000 a month. In other words, $500 more of their income will go toward making the mortgage payments on their old home. To put it another way, they'll have $500 less income with which to qualify for a new home.

If they had a lot of income and the payments on a new mortgage on a new house were small, it probably wouldn't make much difference. But if Helen and Peter were like most people they'd be stretching to get into another property, and they'd need every bit of income in order to qualify for the new mortgage. Reducing their income by $500 might be just enough to keep them from qualifying for the new property.

At this point I can almost hear perceptive readers saying, "Mr. Irwin, you've made a mistake. Their income *won't* go down, because the old house will be rented, presumably for at least $1,000. Therefore, it will make enough to meet it's monthly payment amount. Peter and Helen's income will remain essentially the same."

Logically that would seem to be the case. However, lenders are a wary bunch, particularly these days. They know that rental property investment can be a chancy business. They've heard of vacancies and repair and maintenance problems. Therefore, while they will count all of Helen and Peter's debt, generally they *won't* count all of their income from the rental property.

There are two ways that this is handled. In one method, all of the debt is added to their outstanding debt and all of the income is added to their total income. A wash, right? Unfortunately not. Typically you need a ratio of approximately three times the income to debt. Therefore a debt of $1,000 (from the old house, now refinanced) must have income of $3,000 to offset it. But rental income is only $1,000. By this method they could be way short on income when it comes time to buy a new house.

The other method, currently used more often, is to offset the rental debt by a percentage of rental income. For example, all rental debt is counted when computing the formula for qualifying for a new mortgage. But only 75 percent of rental income is counted. Thus, Peter and Helen's refinance of $1,000-a-month payments is offset only by rental income of $750 a month (their true rental income is $1,000, but only 75 percent can be counted). Thus they end up with an additional debt load of $250. This must be offset three times, meaning they will still need an additional $750 worth of extra income.

If all this sounds complex and arcane, rest assured that it is precisely calculated anytime you get a new mortgage.

Tip

If you have trouble figuring this out, check with a mortgage broker. Let him or her do the calculations for you. They can quickly tell you how refinancing will affect your future ability to borrow.

The Effect of Current Mortgage Market Conditions

Yet another factor to consider before plunging ahead with a refinance of your property is the current mortgage market condition. It's important to remember that mortgage availability, interest rates, and costs vary enormously over time.

In 1982, it was not uncommon to pay as much as 15 percent interest on a fixed, 30-year home mortgage. Ten years later, in 1992, that same mortgage was bearing an interest rate of 8 percent, almost half. There's nothing to say that within another 10 years, or less, rates won't be back up again.

The same holds true for mortgage costs. During times of steep interest, lenders typically want lots of "points" up front. (A point is 1 percent of the mortgage amount.) On the other hand when rates are low, often there may be few or even no points at all to pay. In short, your costs of refinancing will vary, just as will the costs of the mortgage itself.

If you are planning to refinance and buy during a period of high interest rates and high costs, you may want to reconsider. Paying a high interest rate may mean that you will not be able to get as much money as you need out of your property. Or your mortgage payments could be too high.

During periods of high interest rates (and high mortgage costs) it may make better sense simply to sell, and not try to keep your house as a rental. The costs of getting money out by refinancing may simply be too steep for it to be worthwhile.

On the other hand, if you happen to be thinking about doing this during a period of lower rates, you may find that your plans are enhanced by market conditions. A low-interest-rate loan may be just what's needed to help you out of your old property with a workable refinance.

Tip

If you have a good current interest rate on your home mortgage and want to refinance, why not consider a home equity loan? Perhaps your current mortgage is lower than market rates. If you refinanced, you'd end up with a higher first mortgage.

An alternative is a home equity loan. These are widely available, often are amortized (paid back) over 15 years or more, carry competitive interest rates, and, sometimes, the lender is so eager to place them that refinance charges will be waived!

Trap

Beware of adjustables. Adjustable loans are great for the short term. They offer lower interest rates at the beginning (sometimes called "teasers"), but after a year or so their rates often go up higher than you would have paid had you obtained a fixed-interest-rate mortgage.

If you refinance to create a rental property for yourself, presumably you're going to keep that property for a long time. If that's the case, then an adjustable may very well be the wrong kind of loan for you.

Check Out the Neighborhood

It's a simple truth, but the fact is that neighborhoods change. What was once a marvelous area, perfect for raising kids, may quickly have deteriorated into a crime-ridden neighborhood with problems such as drug-dealing and theft. (Perhaps one of the reasons you're moving is to get out of that old neighborhood and into a better one?)

The question you must ask yourself is, "In my neighborhood, would I likely get a good tenant, and would I feel safe and comfortable coming back to collect rents?"

If your answer is yes, then you can comfortably look forward to a nice rental area. On the other hand, if your answer is no, then beware. Your house simply may not be suitable for renting. You may be better off selling and getting rid of the place. I can assure you that there's nothing like a bad neighborhood to complicate rental real estate.

Tip

When you consider your neighborhood, don't just limit yourself to today. Consider trends. What was the neighborhood like five years ago? Ten? Is it getting better, or worse? If it's getting worse, what will it be like 5 or 10 years from now? A neighborhood that's still acceptable today, but is deteriorating, may be unsuitable a couple of years down the road. That's an important consideration.

Trap

Many neighborhoods seem to remain unchanged for years and years. You can go away and come back 20 years later, and they will seem just the same.

My experience, however, is that almost all neighborhoods, even the very finest, have an age factor built in. Eventually they get so old, the buildings get so decrepit, that they start to get run-down. This doesn't necessarily mean that they will deteriorate into places where you wouldn't want to rent or live. Hopefully, buyers will see advantages they may offer (such as larger lots, bigger homes, closer-in locations) and rehabilitate. However, there are no guarantees. Many a fine neighborhood has fallen into ruin simply because it got old and outdated.

Suitability as a Rental Property

For a moment, let's consider your current house by itself. Would it make a good rental?

Contrary to popular wisdom, not all houses make good rentals. Some are ideal for owners to occupy but are terrible as rentals. Let's consider some of the features that may disqualify a house from being a good rental.

Size

The first is size. If your house is too small, you may find you can't get enough rent out of it. Most renters, for example, don't want two-bedroom houses or those with only one bathroom. This is particularly the case if the tenants have children.

Tip

Some tenants, particularly older couples whose children have left, actually look for smaller homes. Of course, they are particularly interested in a lower rent. But if you can afford to rent for less, this type of tenant will often stay a long time and take excellent care of the property.

On the other hand, and although it doesn't happen often, you can have a house that is too big. I once had a rental house with six bedrooms and four baths. It wasn't a mansion, just a very large house.

The trouble was that the only people who wanted to rent it were those who had five active kids or those who wanted to move in two or three families. As a result, it went vacant for longer than normal periods between tenants while I waited for an appropriate tenant.

The ideal rental size for a detached single-family home seems to be three bedrooms and two baths. Smaller than that cuts down your potential rent income. Larger than that means you wait longer to rent up, because you need to get more rent and you tend to get larger families who put more wear and tear on the property.

Age

Younger homes make better rentals. Older homes are less desirable as rental properties.

We'll go into this in far greater detail in Chapter 8, but it's simply the case that the older a property gets, the more maintenance is required. Roofs get older and need to be "tuned" every once in a while. Water heaters, furnaces, air conditioners go out. Washers in faucets start to leak. Floors tend to sag or buckle.

In short, any house over 15 years old is going to need increasing amounts of work. Over 25 years, and the work gets substantial. Over 35, and the work can be overwhelming.

Trap

If you're living in the house, it's an easy matter to fix what goes wrong. For a few cents, you can replace a washer. You may be willing to live with uneven floors. Even if a water heater begins to leak, you can buy one for $150 at a builders' discount store and put it in yourself.

But if it's a rental, it's a different story. You may have to take time off from work, or drive over at night, to fix the washer. If you're too busy, you may have to call a plumber, which could cost $50 to $100 for a job you could easily do yourself for 35 cents in parts.

Uneven floors are a liability risk. If the tenant trips and falls on an uneven floor after complaining about it, you could have a lawsuit on your hands. While you might live with the bad floor, you can't afford to let a tenant do so.

Similarly with a water heater, if it's gas you'll want to get a licensed plumber to put it in. If you put it in and somehow there's a problem with the gas (fire or explosion), no matter how good a job you did, you're in line for a big liability problem.

Condition

What's the condition of your home right now? Is it all freshly painted throughout? Are the carpets in good condition and cleaned? Do all the appliances work perfectly? What about the garage door opener, or the gate at the side of the house?

When you rent, you need to be sure that the place is neat, clean, and in good working order. Neat and clean will help you rent it to good tenants. Good working order means you won't be called every other day by those tenants insisting that you fix something.

If your house is in terrible shape, you may have to consider fixing it up so that it will be rentable.

Tip

If you sell, chances are you will want to fix it up anyway. But remember that fixing it up for sale is just an option. Yes, it probably will mean a quicker sale and a better price. But, I've seen sellers who simply offered their properties "as is."

On the other hand, if you're going to rent, you don't have the option of leaving the house "as is." You must get it ready in order to get a good tenant, and to avoid having to be constantly running back to fix broken items.

Amenities

Certain features make a house a better rental. Others detract from its rentability. Let's consider several, and see how they fit in.

Pool. A pool is considered a plus when you own a home. (However, when you sell it may be a minus, because many families today don't want pool homes.) However, my experience has been that as a rental feature, a pool is a nightmare.

A swimming pool requires constant attention. It must be cleaned weekly during the summer months. Chemicals such as acid, soda ash, and chlorine must be added and kept in precise balance. Water must be added. And the equipment must be kept in running order.

I have had bad luck finding pool services who do great work at this. In my experience, most pool services are more interested in saving money by using fewer chemicals and spending less time at the pool, than in doing a good job. As a result, the tenants always seem to be calling complaining about the pool. Either water isn't clear, or the pump isn't working, or something else is wrong.

On the other hand, in my experience having the tenant take care of the pool is even worse. Many tenants simply don't care, and won't take the time to do a good job. As a result, the pool suffers. But because they are responsible for its upkeep, they often don't report the problems, meaning that in the long term the pool deteriorates even more. (This, often in the face of the fact that they are getting a rent reduction for pool care.)

On the plus side, pool houses generally can be rented quicker, and for more, than non-pool homes. However, chances are you'll hire a pool service to do the work, and this cost will probably offset any additional income the pool might generate for the property.

Trap

Yet another problem with a pool is that is represents a significant liability problem. No matter how careful you are, there's always a chance that a tenant or a tenant's friend could be injured or drowned in the pool. If that happens, you will surely be in line for a lawsuit at the best, criminal prosecution at the worst (if negligence on your part can be shown).

Tip

Most home management companies today suggest that landlords with pools carry at least $300,000 in liability insurance. My suggestion is that you carry far more, at least several million dollars' worth. The cost for more insurance isn't that great, and if you ever need it, you'll be very glad it's there.

My suggestion is that if you have a pool home, you don't convert it to a rental. Sell it, and later buy another home without a pool as a rental. I realize that's a very strong statement to make. But my experiences with pools (and I have had a lot of them) have been almost universally bad.

Spas. A spa (hot tub), a familiar item on the West Coast, is almost always considered a plus when selling a home. I suppose the reason is that its small size (they rarely hold more than 500 gallons of water) make them easy to care for. If you make a disastrous mistake with the chemical balance, you can always toss the water and start off fresh. Besides, most people enjoy the hot water of a spa.

On the other hand, for a rental a spa offers the same problems as does a pool. There is the matter of upkeep. Usually the tenants are responsible for it, and it is far easier to maintain than a pool. But if the tenants don't perform their duties, the spa can quickly deteriorate.

If you have a spa in your current home and it's movable (many are), I suggest you take it with you. Leaving it there will probably help you rent up the property in the short run, but cause you many headaches down the road.

Tip

It's a good idea to check up on a spa house at least every other month, to be sure that the tenants are properly caring for it. It's also a good idea to supply the necessary chemicals to the tenants. (The chemicals aren't expensive for a spa.)

Trap

As with a pool, there is increased liability with a spa, perhaps even more so because of the high water temperatures. Spas can prove to be a health risk if the water temperature is too high, or if young or ill people use them.

Large Yard. Everyone wants a large yard, right? That's usually true with tenants. If you have a property with a large, well-kept yard, you'll probably have a much easier time renting your house.

But you have to ask yourself, who's going to take care of the yard once I move out and the tenants move in? And what are the tenants going to do with my yard?

Large yards require heavy-duty mowing, trimming, fertilizing, and watering. I can guarantee you that a tenant is not going to be anxious to do all that for your property. Yet most lease agreements stipulate that the tenant must take care of the property.

To help ensure that the tenants at least keep the plants alive, many landlords with large properties will pay for the water bills. At the least, this avoids the situation where the tenants don't water the yard because they don't want to run up a high water bill. (This is a real problem in parts of the country that are in a drought situation—see Chapter 4 for more details.)

Yard maintenance, however, is another story. I have had tenants who resolutely promised me they would mow lawns, trim shrubs, and take care of the yard. Yet when I came back a month or so later, I found that nothing had been done.

I don't really blame the tenant for this. I've been a tenant myself, and I didn't particularly want to spend my time and effort cleaning up someone else's property. It's understandable.

Yet another problem is that tenants sometimes won't tell you what they have in mind for your yard. I once had a tenant who, after he had moved into a property I had with a large yard, started up an auto body shop, a clear violation of the lease agreement and city zoning codes. Yet it took me months to get him out, and during that time he ruined much of the garden and left truckloads of junk behind.

In another case, a woman parked an RV as well as several cars on the side lawn of a property I was managing. This again was in clear violation of the lease and of zoning ordinances. Yet she paid the rent precisely on time, and the property owner didn't want to evict her over the problem.

Eventually, however, a neighbor complained and the city fined the owner. When the cars and RV were removed, the lawn had died, as had nearby shrubbery. (I am not against parking RVs in rentals. It's just that there must be an appropriate parking location for them.)

If you currently have a home with a large yard, don't think of it as a plus. Rather, consider it a detracting feature from a rental. It will cost you money in maintenance, and it probably will bring you headaches down the road.

Management

Finally, there is the matter of managing the property. Rentals don't take care of themselves. Someone has to be there to answer the phone when the tenant calls at ten at night to complain of a leaky faucet. Someone has to find the tenant and rent up the property. And someone has to get in there and clean up after the tenant leaves.

Who is that person? If you want to succeed as a landlord, most of the time that person will have to be you.

Yes, you can hire a management firm to do all of the above. But it will cost you big bucks. A good property management firm charges you 10 percent of your rental income as a fee. That's just for finding tenants, collecting the rent, and fielding problems. All other costs, such as fixing garbage disposals, cleaning trash, painting after tenants leave, are billed separately and usually at going market rates.

What this means is that you could potentially end up spending 25 percent or more of your rental income, over time, on management (and managed maintenance). And that doesn't include lost income during vacancies.

Note: I am not criticizing property management firms. I have owned and operated them myself. Most are competently run, and do a true service for property owners. All I mean to point out here is the cost difference between doing the job yourself and hiring someone else to do it for you. When you have only one piece of rental property, the costs of hiring someone else to do everything for you are, in many cases, simply prohibitive.

Trap

Remember that the property management firm gets paid whether your property is rented or vacant. There is nothing more frustrating than to get a bill from a property management firm when your house is un-rented!

On the other hand, if you fix a leaky faucet yourself, it probably costs you less than a dollar in parts. If you replace a broken garbage disposal, it only costs you for the disposal and parts, usually around $40, rather than the $150 or more you would pay to have a plumber install it.

Similarly, if you run the ad, show the property, and find the tenant, your costs are minimal. If you handle tenant complaints, your costs are basically only your own time. If you have a management firm do it, costs can be substantial.

It's for these reasons that I suggest the smart way of thinking of a rental conversion is as a part-time job or a hobby. Plan on doing it yourself. Plan on spending a few hours a week on it. (Unfortunately, those hours may tend to be at inconvenient times.) If you do, you'll find that your property will continue to shine, and your rental income should flow in.

Trap

Beware of owning rental property at a distance. Perhaps the biggest mistake you can make in converting to a rental is to then buy a home in a distant city.

You can take good care of your property only if you are living nearby and are able to respond quickly to problems. For example, if you con-vert your current home to a rental and then move 20 or 30 minutes across town, you are still close enough to handle emergencies, such as leaky water heaters and tenant rent-ups. You can still place an ad with your number and respond to rental inquiries. If work such as painting needs to be done after a tenant moves out, you can get over to the house and do it in the evenings or on weekends.

On the other hand if you move far away, you will be forced to rely on a property management firm. And your hoped-for breakeven (or profit, if you're lucky) will tend to disappear.

Tip

Distance is perception. If you're 10 minutes away from your rental property, you won't mind going over to it so much. If you're 30 minutes away, on the other hand, it becomes a hassle. Move an hour away and it's a big, big chore. Move two hours away and it becomes extremely dif-ficult to take care of the property. Move more than two hours away and it becomes impossible.

Should You Convert Your Home to a Rental?

You'll have to weigh the benefits over the negatives. Here's a list that may help you to make the decision:

Benefits of Conversion

- You keep your old house and, hopefully, get appreciation as its value goes up.

- You also get a new house and, hopefully, appreciation on it as its value goes up. (You double your potential profits.)

- You may get a decent tax write-off from your old property.

- You get the ability to write off taxes and mortgage payments on your new house.

Drawbacks of Conversion

- Increasing debt on the old property may decrease your chances of qualifying for a new loan on the new property

- Current mortgage market conditions (interest rates) may not be favorable for a conversion.

- You may not be able to rent your old house for enough money to pay for your basic costs.

- Your old house may not be suitable as a rental property.

- The rental market in your area may be poor.

- You will have to stay close and manage the property yourself.

6

Inspection Pitfalls When Buying

Have you ever seen an advertisement for a piece of electronics equipment, such as a VCR or camcorder, at a discount dealer that looked too good to be true? Perhaps the price was hundreds lower than anywhere else.

So you ran out there and bought yourself what was a real bargain. Or was it?

Perhaps further investigation would have revealed that the unit really was last year's model. Or perhaps its features were obsolete compared with the new models. Or, in the worst case, it might turn out that the model had some defect that required it be sent back to the factory for repairs, perhaps more than once, and that took a lot of time and a lot of mailing expense.

In short, maybe the bargain wasn't such a bargain after all.

The same thing applies with an investment property. Sometimes we can be blinded by low price or by great terms and purchase a property that we really would have been better off passing on. In this chapter we're going to take a look at what you should do before you buy, to make sure you know what you're getting. Here, we're going to consider property inspections before the sale from the buyer/investor's perspective.

Personal Inspection Versus Professional

I can recall appearing as a guest on Sonny Block's syndicated radio talk show (where he discusses real estate and other investments) and having a small disagreement over inspections. I suggested that perhaps an inspection wasn't always worthwhile.

Sonny wisely took issue with this, pointing out that he favored inspections as a way for a home buyer to be more informed about what he or she was buying. I went on to clarify what I meant.

I favor inspections too, but the problem I've found is that sometimes home inspectors don't do a wonderful job for the buyer. For example, sometimes home inspectors give a false sense of security by telling a buyer that a property is "OK" when in reality it may have one or more serious defects. Other times you're better off with a builder or specialist who can not only point out defects but also suggest solutions.

In other words, I don't think you can simply go down a phone book list of home inspectors, pick one out, have the inspection, and feel that you've done all you can. It takes more than that.

Trap

While home inspection has become a part of virtually every real estate purchase as of this writing, most states still do not license home inspectors. What this means is that almost anyone can hang out a shingle as one. As a result, if you simply hire a "home inspector" you can't be sure of the quality of the inspection you'll get. Until your state licenses and regulates home inspectors, you must be as wary of the inspector as of the property.

Tip

Professional organizations are now being formed to upgrade the performance of inspectors. ASHI, or the American Society of Home Inspectors, is one such group. You may want to check to see that your inspector is a member of ASHI.

History of Home Inspection

For years, the rule in real estate was "Buyer beware." It was up to the buyer to determine what he or she was purchasing and to make sure that it was a sound product.

This system worked surprisingly well in the vast majority of cases. Occasionally, however, a seller would conceal a serious defect in a property, such as a cracked foundation, or broken/leaking water pipes, or some other defect. Sometimes these problems could be threatening to life or health, as in faulty wiring or leaking gas lines.

The result was a series of lawsuits across the country, where buyers sued sellers for selling defective properties. Since, in most cases, the sellers had been represented by a real estate agent, the agents were also named in the suits.

Even though the agents protested that they were innocent of any knowledge of the defects in the property, they were often faced with paying for lengthy litigation. As a result, selling agents began to suggest that buyers obtain the services of an inspector to determine the true condition of the property (as was sometimes already being done in commercial and industrial real estate). Thus, if something later proved to be defective, the buyer couldn't easily come back and successfully sue the seller and agent. That inspection often was used to demonstrate that the buyer had had the opportunity to gain full knowledge about the property.

Thus, the home inspection's purpose initially was to protect the seller, not the buyer!

Enter Disclaimers

Along the way, as an added protection to the seller, agents began to suggest that sellers formally disclose any known defects in the property to the buyers. Today several states, including California, have codified this requirement, and many more will soon do so.

Thus when you buy a home today, whether for rental or for living in, you are likely to get a long list of disclaimers from the seller. This may disclose to you anything from a cracked driveway or broken slab to asbestos in heating ducts or a leaky roof. When you get this disclaimer, informative though it may be, keep in mind that what it's doing, in part, is protecting the seller. It's making sure that you know about a problem and thus can't come back later on, to claim that someone sold you something other than represented. It's giving you full disclosure as to the nature of the product (house) you're purchasing.

Tip

When I sell a property I always disclose everything, even some things that might only be possibilities. Remember, for the seller, the purpose of the disclaimer is to get everything out into the open, so that he or she can't later be held liable for concealing a defect.

Thus you, as a buyer, must not always be alarmed by the disclaimer you are given. Often even very minor problems may be disclaimed, problems that should cause you no concern. Knowing how to read between the lines of the disclaimer is almost as important as getting it.

Today when you buy a property you can expect to receive both a disclaimer (sometimes from the seller as well as from each agent involved) and a written suggestion from the selling agent and the seller that you hire your own inspector to take a close look at the property. If you hire an inspector, then you'll have trouble going back later on to claim that you didn't know about a defect. If you refuse to hire an inspector, then the seller can claim that you had the opportunity to look more closely at the property but chose not to, hence you have no right to complain after the sale.

From Your Perspective

Thus far we've been looking at how inspections and disclosures help the seller. Now let's turn 180 degrees and see how they help you, the buyer. They help in two ways.

First, a thorough inspection of a property you are purchasing can indeed reveal defects that you might otherwise not have known about. These defects may make you change your mind about purchasing the property.

Tip

In some states, you have a certain time period within which to gracefully back out of a sale after you have been given the seller's and agent's disclosures. The time limit in California, for example, is three days.

Also, most buyers today condition the purchase on their approval of an inspection within a reasonable amount of time, say 10 days. What this means is that in reality you have 10 days in which to inspect the house. If during that time you decide it has something wrong with it that you don't like, you can back out, get back your deposit, and have no more commitment to the deal.

The second way an inspection can aid you is in leveraging the seller. An inspection can reveal defects of which even the seller may not be aware. For example, the inspector may climb into the attic and discover a broken joist or frayed electrical wiring. You may then say you don't want the property unless and until the seller fixes the problem, or lowers the price to compensate for your costs in fixing it.

One buyer I met recently was purchasing a home located on a hillside. To all appearances, the home seem perfectly well constructed and secure on its foundation.

However, an inspection revealed that parts of the foundation had been undermined by runoff from winter rains and would have to be repaired, a potentially expensive proposition. The buyers pointed this out to the seller and said they wouldn't take the house as originally agreed. But they were willing to renegotiate a price based on this new information. Eventually, the seller sold the property for a third less! The buyers purchased, and then were able to correct the problem fairly easily, thus saving themselves a lot of money.

Taking Part in the Inspection Process

Since the onus is on you, the buyer, to do the inspection, it's important that it be thorough and appropriate. In other words, since it's up to you to find out what the problems are (over and above what a seller and an agent may disclose), you want to be sure to get the right kind of inspection. How do you do this?

My first suggestion is that, above and beyond anything else you do, you inspect the property yourself. You are the person most concerned with the purchase, therefore you shouldn't leave it entirely up to others to tell you what you're buying.

Please note that I'm not suggesting that it be *only* you who inspects the property. What I am saying is that you should conduct as thorough an inspection as possible yourself.

But, you may argue, I don't know very much about houses. What could I hope to uncover?

The answer is, all sorts of things. You can easily tell if there are visible cracks over doorways and windows, suggesting foundation problems. You can tell if the floor is uneven when you walk over it. You can see if faucets are leaking, or if there are wet spots under sinks. You can see if shingles have blown off the roof, or if the siding on the house is peeling. There are so many things that are obvious to anyone who looks closely that you won't have trouble finding many of them.

Further, assuming that you're not a builder yourself, or someone who is thoroughly familiar with properties, you should accompany any inspector you hire. For example, I recently purchased a home that had some obvious water problems in the air space between the floor and the ground. (It had no basement, only about an 18-inch crawl space.)

I wanted the inspector to get down into the crawl space and look at every square foot of it. He did, and I followed right behind, listening to everything he could tell me, which was quite a bit. By looking at discoloration on boards, he determined the high-water mark. By examining the cracked soil he determined that the problem was recurring, probably every winter. By examining the underside of the floor he determined that there was no dry rot or other damage because of it. I was right there with him, looking at everything he had to point out, and learning quite a bit. As a result, I was able to point out to the seller that the house needed substantial improvements in its yard drainage, and the price was adjusted downward accordingly.

My point, however, is that by going right along with the inspector, I was able to see the problem, learn what it was, and feel confident about what could be done to correct it.

Tip

Active participation is the watchword when you are buying property (or anything else, for that matter). Don't hesitate to get right in there and see for yourself. Never just take anyone else's word for it.

Using the Right Inspector

Assuming that you're going to hire someone to help you with your house inspection, it's critical that you hire the appropriate inspector. When you are buying for investment purposes, this is doubly important.

Investors often buy properties that are run-down or that have defects, simply because they can be purchased for lower prices. The idea here is that you'll purchase for a very low price, fix the defect, and then sell for a substantial profit.

Thus, you actually want the inspector to perform two functions. The first we've already discussed, the finding and revealing of problems. His second function is to suggest methods for remedying these.

My own experience is that, while those who advertise themselves as home inspectors may indeed be able to uncover most potential defects, frequently they are very inadequate when it comes to suggesting solutions. For example, a friend recently was purchasing a home that had a crack in the slab. The property was on level ground, but that ground was primarily made up of clay. During the dry summer months, the moisture in the clay decreased and it shrank in size. During the winter rains, when the ground under the slab became moist, it absorbed water and expanded. The continual contraction and expansion of the soil under the slab, over the years, had eventually broken the cement in several places. This was readily visible, and a home inspector pointed it out.

When my friend, however, asked the inspector what if anything could be done about it, the inspector just shrugged and said, "The cracks could open up wider, the floor could shift, with one side moving higher than another, or in the worst case, the house could separate and possibly fall down."

These were pretty grim scenarios and my friend was really upset, almost as much as were the sellers, who saw a deal fading away. I suggested that perhaps what was needed was to get someone in there who had a lot of experience with cracked slabs and that particular kind of soil. The suggestion was made to consult with a soil engineer, a person who specializes in analyzing soil problems.

I suggested that even this was probably not the best move. The soil engineer would undoubtedly confirm that there was expansive soil, and simply reinforce what the inspector had said about its destructive potential. However, what my friend was looking for was solutions, not a rehash of old problems. Thus, I indicated that a contractor who specializes in drainage and in cracked-slab repair might be in order.

My buyer contacted such a person, and she examined the property. While confirming the original diagnosis of the problem, she went on to point out that by using proper drainage, perhaps even a sump pump, the water in winter could be kept away from under the slab. If the dirt under the slab was kept dry, it wouldn't expand.

Once thus stabilized, the existing cracks in the slab could be treated as cosmetic problems. (There were steel reinforcing bars in the cement to keep the slab from moving further.) The cracks could be patched and forgotten about. The cost of the drainage was under $1,000, and the patching was under $100. The seller agreed to pay for these corrections, and the deal was made with all parties satisfied. (Note: The contractor pointed out that she frequently bought similar properties at deep discounts from sellers who just wanted out from under the problem. Then she made the corrections, resold the property, and walked off with substantial profits.)

My point here is that the right inspector can make a world of difference.

Tip

You want two things in an inspector, only one of which is the ability to determine defects and problems. The other essential element is the ability to suggest solutions.

Finding the Right Inspector for the Problem

Where do you find the right inspector, the one who will give you *solutions* to possible problems?

My suggestion is that you use whatever resources are available to you, including recommendations by not only your (the buyer's) agent, but the seller's as well. You may also want to rely on recommendations by others in the field and, as a last resort, the yellow pages of the phone book.

As you buy and sell more properties in a given area, you will develop relationships with those in a variety of fields and will begin to create your own "black book" of tradespeople whom you can rely upon to help you when making a decision as to the quality of a property. If you're just starting out, however, I would suggest you consider a two-step process.

The first step should be to have an inspection by someone who is a generalist. Unless you already know of a problem, your first concern should be discovery. You want to uncover any potential defects in the property.

Then, once you know about defects, you can call in a second person to evaluate them and give you suggestions for correction. This would be a specialist.

Tip

Think of the analogy of medicine. When you are sick you usually go first to see a generalist, a GP who can narrow down the problem. Once that's done, the GP may send you to a specialist for treatment. Do the same thing when it comes to the inspection of a house.

Yes, this means it will cost you for more than one inspection. But in the long run it could save you a great deal of money and many headaches.

Here's a list of potential inspectors who can help you make buying decisions:

- Generalists:

  General contractor

  Home inspector

  Structural engineer

- Specialists:

  Civil engineer

Drainage specialist

Electrical contractor

Grading contractor

Heating/Air Conditioning contractor

Lath and plaster contractor

Paving contractor

Plasterer

Plumbing contractor

Roofing contractor

Soil engineer

Structural engineer

Written Reports

Once you have your inspector, you then need to get a report that you can use. We've already discussed one kind of report, verbal. As you go along with the inspector, he or she will point out the various features and problems of the house. You can see for yourself what's being described and you can make an on-the-spot evaluation.

However, even more important may be the written report that will follow. This should be prepared by the inspector and delivered to you within a few days.

The written report will undoubtedly go over much of what was pointed out verbally. However, in addition it should also include any evaluations and recommendations that the inspector makes after the inspection.

Tip

There are two good reasons for the written report. First, it includes recommendations that weren't made at the time of the inspection, as well as those that were made but that you may have forgotten. Second, it can be used as a tool to get the seller to lower the price or to pay for the correction of defects. It's one thing to verbally tell a seller that this or that is wrong and needs repair. It's quite another to hand the seller a formal report from an independent third party that spells it out in writing.

It's important that the written report be in a form that's usable by you. What you're looking for is a report that is both comprehensive and detailed. You want to know that everything has been covered, and that you have been given all the specifics.

Trap

Some inspectors rely too heavily on computer-generated reports. There are several programs out there that allow an inspector to simply key-board the answers to a series of questions. Then the computer generates the report.

What you end up with are several pages of computer paper with stock phrases. You're getting back a form prepared for everyone, when what you want is information created specifically for you and your property.

Tip

Before hiring an inspector, ask about the written report. Ask if it's a nar-rative (written out by the inspector for your specific property), or com-puter-generated. Beware of reports that are exclusively computer-gen-erated.

Off-Property Reports

Finally, there is one last kind of inspection you may want to consider, and that is one which is not conducted at the property. What I'm speak-ing of here are reports on such things as seismic activity, runoff, flood-ing, tornadoes, hurricanes, and so forth. Depending on where the prop-erty is located, it may be affected by a wide variety of such outside influences.

Usually, if the property is in a flood or seismic zone, the seller will disclaim this, but not always. My suggestion is that you ask the agent involved, or an agent in the area if you are dealing directly with the seller, if there are any external problems that you should know about.

Typically agents will be well aware of any such concerns, because they have to deal with them in property they sell.

If you learn of any such problems, I don't suggest you go out and pay to have someone do a report on them for you. That could be pro-hibitively expensive.

What you may want to do, however, is to contact local government organizations such as the city or county building and planning depart-ments, to learn if such reports have been done. If they have been done they are normally public property, and for a nominal fee you can obtain one.

Why is this necessary?

Consider. Some properties may be lying in a flood plain. You may be purchasing in the summertime and a river, which could be miles away, would never occur to you as presenting a problem of any kind.

But in winter, that river could rise. Under certain conditions, perhaps a storm that would likely occur only once every 10 or even every 50 years, that river could breach its banks and flood the surrounding countryside, including your home.

As a result, you might lose the property. Further, you might be required to carry flood insurance on the property in order to get financing. And the cost of such insurance might be prohibitively high. In fact, once you consider the danger, you may want to get the seller to reduce the price, or you may not even want to purchase the property at all!

I once was considering purchasing a property on the west coast that was at the base of a lovely mountain. I was buying directly from the seller, and she kept telling me how beautiful the view of the mountain was and I whole-heartedly agreed.

However, I chanced to ask a local broker if there were any problems special to that area that I should know about.

I distinctly remember him scratching his head, shaking it, and then saying, "Not unless you mean that volcano over there." He was pointing at the beautiful mountain!

Of course, it hadn't erupted in the past 40 years. But that's just a blink of an eye in geologic time.

It always pays to check out the "lay of the land" when you buy. Get that "other" report or inspection. You know, it's the one you keep putting off, or just don't have time to get around to.

7

Dealing Fairly
but Strongly
with Tenants

Tenants are both your greatest asset and your greatest liability when it comes to owning investment real estate. Without tenants, you wouldn't have the income to make payments and couldn't hang on to the property. Yet bad tenants can make owning a piece of property a living hell.

In this chapter we're going to discuss how to deal with residential tenants. The assumption is that you own a single-family house, condo, townhouse, or co-op. The goal is not only to learn how to deal with tenant problems, but to anticipate them and head them off.

An Investment in Tenants

As soon as you acquire investment real estate, you're going to enter the wonderful world of property management. You'll need to find good solid tenants who are willing and able to make the monthly rent payments and who will take care of your property.

As those who rent on a regular basis know, this is usually not a problem. I have found most people, including tenants, to be honest and reliable. I have had tenants who have left the property cleaner than when they moved in. I have had tenants who paid their rent a few days ahead of schedule just to be sure it arrived on time. I've had tenants who have fixed broken plumbing themselves when they knew it was inconvenient for me to get out there, and then charged only for the parts. Overall, I have found good tenants to be the rule, rather than the exception.

However, this chapter is dedicated to those times when the tenant isn't so wonderful. If you rent long enough, you will eventually run into the bad tenant. Here you'll get some help on dealing with him or her.

Renting Up

Protecting yourself begins when you first rent up a property. What you do at the beginning will often determine how things turn out at the end. (Note: This chapter is not intended as a complete course in property management. Rather, we're just going to touch on the sensitive areas. For a more detailed explanation I suggest you read *The McGraw-Hill Property Management Handbook*, 1986.)

Qualifying the Tenant

There are lots of ways to qualify tenants, that is to make sure that they are who they say they are, that they have a good track record of making payments and taking care of the property in which they live. We'll discuss two here.

The first is to contact the previous landlord. To my way of thinking, this is the single most important phone call you can make with regard to tenants. You want to check with a landlord from whom these tenants have previously rented. Hopefully this person will tell you how well they maintained the property, how well they paid the rent, and so forth.

Trap

Don't bother contacting the tenants' current landlord. If the tenants are bad, he or she is likely to give you a marvelous recommendation, just to help get the tenants out! The current landlord is the last person you want to contact.

Tip

Contact the landlord prior to the present one. The tenants will have already left this landlord behind, and he or she shouldn't have any reason to give them a more favorable, or less favorable, report than they deserve. In fact, if the tenants were bad (didn't pay the rent, left a mess, etc.), this landlord is very likely to lay it all on you. You'll get your clearest information here.

In my rental application, I always ask for the name of the landlord prior to the current one. I specify that if the prospective tenants refuse to list this prior landlord's name, I will refuse to rent to them.

The second important item to get is a credit report. This will give you a brief history of the prospective tenants' background with regard to paying debts. The rule is, you don't want to rent to a deadbeat, a tenant who chronically and across the board doesn't make payments.

Credit reports are easy to obtain. Look in the phone book for credit-reporting services (they are listed) and call up one or two. If for some reason there isn't a credit agency in your area, see if there's a local landlords' organization. Typically these have agreements with credit-reporting agencies and can supply you with a report. The reports cost about $35, if they are written. If you want only an oral report (where you are read the information over the phone), the charge can be much less.

Tip

I personally don't always follow the rules. One tenant I rented to had the worst credit report I'd ever seen. She appeared to have been late or defaulted on every loan she ever took out. Yet she explained this as a series of problems with her former husband, wherein he had run up bills and then left her to pay them off. She had been unable to do so.

She seemed honest and sincere. She had a steady job, and she assured me that if she couldn't pay the rent, she would move out. I believed her and rented her the house. She turned out to be one of the best tenants I've ever had, keeping the place spotless and always paying the rent on time. Eventually, after two years, she did run into some hard times and, true to her word, she moved out without a problem when she couldn't pay.

Trap

Be sure you get the tenants' written permission, in the rental application, to run a credit check. They shouldn't object to this. To run the check you will also need some minimal information such as name, current address, social security number, and driver's license. (It has always amazed me how easy it is to get a credit check on almost anyone!)

Rental Application Form

This is just a form that asks for pertinent information, such as former landlords, bank accounts, and credit history. I suggest you contact a large property management firm in your area for one of these. They will use them extensively, and more than likely will be happy to let you have one. You can then use it as your model.

The Rental Agreement

Once you've determined that you've got good prospective tenants, the next thing is to sign them up. For this you need a rental agreement.

There are two types of rental agreements. A lease is for a set period of time, typically a year, and generally implies that you get first and last month's rent up front. It is for the total amount of money of the term. For example, a 12-month lease at $1,000 a month is for $12,000. A month-to-month rental agreement is just what it says. You get the first month's rent in advance (plus usually a cleaning deposit) and the rent is paid monthly. Either you or the tenant can give 30 days' notice to terminate the rental.

Most novice landlords immediately opt for the lease. They look at that legal-appearing document that commits the tenant to a long chunk of time and think that will ensure that the tenant pays the rent and keeps the place up. They also like getting two months' rent up front.

The problem, however, is that if the tenant decides to move out, you can get your money only by suing, and then only as the rent comes due. It's often far easier to simply forget it and rent to a new tenant.

Trap

In some respects, residential leases protect the tenant more than the landlord. If the tenant moves out, it's difficult if not impossible to enforce the terms of the lease. On the other hand, the lease protects the tenant from rent raises and the sale of the property by you, the landlord.

There's also the matter of the first and last month's rent, usually paid up front in a lease. However, this can actually work against you. By the time the last month rolls around, the tenant realizes that the rent is already paid. Further, there's no incentive to leave the place clean. As a result, a straight lease too often results in the tenant's moving out and leaving the premises a mess.

The Security/Cleaning Deposit

As a result, landlords who have been around a while focus on the cleaning/security deposit. ("Cleaning" refers to the deposit held against the tenant's leaving the place clean; "security" refers to the deposit held against the tenant's not paying rent. There is usually one combined deposit for both purposes.) This is money that the tenant pays up front and that the landlord holds until after the tenant has moved out. If the place is left clean and if all the rent has been paid, the tenant gets it back. If not, the tenant pays for damages and unpaid rent from the deposit. Most experienced landlords realize that a big security deposit is far more important than the last month's rent.

Some states limit the size of the security/cleaning deposit. In California, for example, it cannot be more than twice a single month's rent.

Tip

Some landlords try to get both first and last month's rent, plus a big security deposit. The problem here is that unless the rental market is really tight and there are just no places to rent, most tenants will balk at forking over so much cash up front. For example, if the rent is $1,000 a month and the security deposit is also $1,000, the tenant needs to come up with $3,000 just to move in (first and last month's rent, plus security deposit). Many tenants simply don't have that much cash.

A compromise that I have been using is to get the first month's rent (an absolute necessity) plus a big cleaning/security deposit. I still use a lease form, but I don't worry about that last month's rent. By the time the last month has come around, if the tenant is still there and paying it shouldn't be a problem.

A snag can sometimes occur with tenants who are wary of the landlord not returning the cleaning/security deposit. They will refuse to pay the last month's rent. They will say something such as, "Take the last month's rent out of the security/cleaning deposit."

Beware of this, for if you agree you undermine the whole purpose of the security/cleaning deposit—to ensure that the place is left clean and the rent is paid.

Tip

I always notify tenants up front, in the rental agreement in big type, that the security/cleaning deposit cannot be used for the last month's rental payment. Further, if a tenant asks to have this done, I refuse. If a tenant insists, I inform them that I will consider them nonpaying unless they come forth with the rent, and will report them as such to a credit-reporting agency. If your tenants are concerned about their credit, as they should be, they will comply.

Trap

In most states, as this is being written, a security/cleaning deposit that you receive on a rental from a tenant can be deposited into your personal account. However, the laws are changing. Soon you may be required to keep that security/cleaning deposit in a separate checking account, and even to pay interest on it to the tenant.

Keeping the money separate is a good idea. Too often I've seen landlords spend the security/cleaning deposit and then, when the tenant moves out, not have the money available to pay them back!

Pets

This is a huge problem with rentals. People have pets. (I have several myself.) However, pets that are not carefully trained can cause thousands of dollars of damage to a rental.

For example, a friend of mine recently rented a home to a couple who said they had one dog. It turned out they had two, but after they showed my friend a litter box and said how careful they were with the animals, she agreed to this.

It was a mistake. When they moved, she discovered that they had allowed the animals to urinate on the carpeting in most rooms of the home. Animal urine usually is not removable. The carpets and padding were a complete loss and had to be replaced.

Of course, she had the security/cleaning deposit. However, the existing carpeting was seven or eight years old, and in good conscience she had to depreciate it. As a result their deposit only paid for about a third of the cost of putting in new carpeting. Yes, she did end up with new carpeting. But it cost her plenty, and it was an expense she hadn't counted on.

Pets are wonderful, but they can cause terrible damage to a rental if they are not properly trained and cared for. If you can find tenants without pets, you will have far less wear and tear, on average, to your property.

Trap

I think it's usually a mistake to specify when renting that you won't accept pets. The reason is that the tenants may tell you, when they move in, that they don't have pets. But a few weeks or months later, you discover that they have "acquired" a pet. It's best to deal with this up front and say you allow pets, but try to restrict the number and kind.

I have a friend who operates a property management service, and he says people with pets are always telling him, "If you rent to us, we'll get rid of our pet." He replies, "I wouldn't rent to anyone who would get rid of a pet."

Tip

Dealing with a pet can simply be a matter of increasing the security/cleaning deposit. If there's enough money at stake, the tenants will make sure the place is kept clean. If they don't, you'll have the funds to fix it.

The problem is that in a rental market where there are lots of vacancies, you may not be able to get a big enough security/cleaning deposit. Or, as noted earlier, there may be governmental restrictions on how big a cleaning/security deposit you can charge.

Children

Years ago landlords used to say with a smirk, "I love children. Just not in my rental."

They don't do that much anymore. Today it's usually not possible to restrict a rental unit on the basis of children. If you refuse to rent to someone solely because they have kids, you might find yourself on the end of an anti-discrimination lawsuit.

The problem is that children are children. They tend to write on walls, kick floorboards, break windows with baseballs, and on and on. I did it. You did it. All children tend to do it. Which is to say, they are hard on rental property. However, that's just the way things are. If you're in the rental business, you'll probably have to put up with the wear and tear that children cause.

Besides, children have to live somewhere, and if you have a big security/cleaning deposit and make it clear up front that you expect the parents to take care of the premises, you probably won't have a big problem.

Of course, you may purchase a property in an "adults only" community where no children are allowed. However, these are usually reserved for retirement areas, and rentals there tend to be few and far between.

Number of Tenants

Of more concern are the number of tenants who inhabit your rental. In uncertain economic times, as is the case as this is written, it becomes increasingly hard for a family to make ends meet. Thus it's not uncommon for parents to take back grown children. Sometimes these children are married and have children of their own.

Tip

Your rental agreement should always specify the number of occupants allowed in the premises, and should list them by name.

As a result, you may start out with one family renting your home and end up with two or more. Instead of the three or four tenants you bargained for, you may find eight or ten living in the property.

This can be a serious problem. Overuse of the property can result in damage and wear and tear much faster than with the normal complement of tenants. Further, many municipalities have passed regulations limiting the number of tenants who may occupy a property, just to prevent this from happening. Thus, you may be subject to fines.

Trap

Keep track of how many people are in your rental property. Laws regulating the number of tenants allowed per rental unit are springing up all over the country. The problem is that there are no good guidelines. Cities and other governing boards have found that it's difficult to tell just how many tenants should occupy a building. Maximum occupancy, as determined by fire and safety department rules, usually comes down to the maximum number the floor joists can hold, or that can safely be evacuated in case of fire. By these rules, the maximum number is often 5 or 10 per room! Thus, cities and counties have taken to arbitrarily limiting the number of people they allow, sometimes in a very restrictive way. As a result many of these rules are being challenged in court, and, indeed, some are being found unconstitutional.

Evicting a family when too many people have moved in can be hard. For one thing, in these cases the tenants typically pay the rent promptly and right on time, and thus you aren't motivated to evict them.

For another, it's often difficult to tell how many people are actually living in a property. No matter when you drop by, the tenants may say that these are just friends or relatives who are staying for a few days and will be leaving shortly. It's difficult to pin them down as to how many people are actually living in the property.

Tip

One way to keep tab on the number of occupants is to drive by at night to see how many cars are regularly parked in the driveway or on the adjacent street. Another is to schedule a series of "walk-through inspections" with the tenants. (Your rental agreement should provide that you have access to the property not only in an emergency, but also with proper notice, usually 24 hours.) Check the closets. Often different inhabitants will separate their clothing and it becomes pretty easy to tell. Nevertheless, it's still usually difficult to regulate the number of tenants occupying your property, no matter what you do.

Tenants Who Break Things

Sometimes things get broken while a tenant is in the property. For example, I recently had a tenant whose son couldn't keep his baseball away from the back windows. Every month, it seemed a different window was broken.

The problem was that the windows were large and, hence, were of safety plate glass. As a result, instead of the 20 or 30 dollars is would normally cost to get a window fixed, these cost several hundred dollars apiece.

The first time it happened the tenant let me know, and I told them that since their son had broken the window they were responsible for fixing it, and that it should be fixed quickly before it became a safety problem. I went by the property the next week and, sure enough, it had been fixed. However, the tenant complained of the high cost.

The next time it happened, the tenant didn't tell me. Instead, a gardener informed me that there was glass lying on the back deck. I came by, and sure enough another window had been broken. The glass on the ground had been cleaned up. However, the window had not been replaced. Rather, the tenants had covered the remaining sharp pieces of glass with plastic stick tape. They had done a good job, so that the entire area of the window was covered.

However, I informed them that it was still a definite safety hazard. I told them that they had to fix it. If it wasn't fixed within a month I would hire a window company to come and fix it, and I would take the cost out of their security/cleaning deposit. Then their rent would be raised, to bring their security/cleaning deposit back up to its previous level.

Tip

It's a good idea to have a clause in your rental agreement that provides for temporarily raising the rent to bring the security/cleaning deposit back up to its original level after any money from it has been spent.

The third time this happened, the tenants called and said they were moving. They said they couldn't afford to keep replacing windows in my house.

I told them that it would be simpler to remove their son's ball and bat, but if they really wanted to move, I wouldn't hold them to the lease. However, in order to get their cleaning/security deposit back, they would have to pay rent until I found another tenant, and leave the premises as clean as they had found them. They reconsidered, and as of this writing are still living there. There have been no more broken windows.

Tenants Who Won't Pay Their Rent

Thus far the problems we've been discussing have been relatively minor, in the sense that they haven't jeopardized the landlord's ability to continue making mortgage, tax, interest, and other payments on the property. Things, however, turn decidedly more serious when the tenant won't or can't pay the rent.

In most cases tenants who don't pay rent have run into a financial roadblock. They may be shouldering a sudden financial burden, such as a sick relative, to whom they channel the funds they would normally use for rent. Or they may have lost income because they have been laid off from work. Sometimes tenants are simply poor managers of money and have gotten into too much debt; instead of paying the rent, they pay their Mastercard, Visa, and other credit lines instead. (Robbing Peter—you, the landlord—to pay Paul.)

When your tenants do not pay rent, my suggestion is that you as a landlord should immediately adopt a three-step approach. The first step is to confront the tenants and insist they pay the rent immediately. The second step is to determine if the problem the tenants are having is likely to be temporary or permanent. The third step is to decide how long you're going to wait before you take action.

Steps in Collecting Rent

The steps I have just mentioned require some further explanation. The steps are:

Confrontation

Determining if the problem is temporary

Deciding when to take action

Confrontation

Usually rents are paid on the first of the month. (Any day will do, of course, but the first of the month is usually most convenient for both landlord and tenant.)

Some landlords make it a point to stop by on the first and personally collect the rent. This, of course, is the surest way of knowing if you're going to get it or if there's a problem. For my rentals, I always have the tenants mail the rent in. It's just more convenient for me.

Trap
___
Never buy a rental property in an area where you're personally afraid to go to collect the rent at any time of the day or evening. If you do you're just asking for trouble, and the day will surely come when the tenant doesn't pay and you'll feel too uncomfortable to go down there and demand payment. *Then* what do you do?

Tip
___
If you're going to have tenants mail the rent to you, be sure you emphasize, both orally and in the rental agreement, that they should send the money several days in advance of the due date in order to compensate for the time it takes the postal service to deliver it.

A good idea is to prepare and give to the tenant a series of twelve envelopes, pre-addressed and pre-stamped, for each month's rent. You can also write on the envelope the day it is to be mailed. In this fashion you won't have to worry about comments from the tenant such as, "I couldn't find a stamp," or "I forgot when to put it into the mail."

If the rent is due the first of the month and I don't get it on time, I usually wait until the third before calling a tenant to see what's the problem. If the tenant has previously been a regular on-time payer, the usual answer is that it was mailed and just hasn't arrived yet, or he or she forgot to drop it into the mail or some such thing. Typically, in such a circumstance, a phone call is all that's needed. The check usually arrives within the next two days.

Tip

Sometimes you have to make exceptions for an exceptional tenant. For one property, I have a tenant who has been there for several years, keeps the property spotless, and has never failed to pay the rent. However, she receives her income from government retirement checks and they are sometimes as much as two weeks late. Consequently, her checks to me are sometimes also as much as two weeks late.

I don't call and I don't complain. I feel confident I'll get my money, and I'm willing to wait the extra time because I want to keep her as a tenant.

Sometimes going the extra mile for a good tenant is far wiser than insisting your rent be paid absolutely on time.

Five Days and No Rent

For a tenant who has previously paid on time, but now hasn't responded within two days to your phone call, a personal visit is absolutely necessary. You need to stop by and confront the tenants. Usually around dinner time is best, because you're most likely to catch the tenants at home.

Tip

Confrontation, unfortunately, is a part of collecting back rent. If you're not willing to put yourself out there and demand what's due you, don't expect it to suddenly just appear. Personally, I have never been particularly good at confrontation. As a consequence, when dealing with a recalcitrant tenant I carefully rehearse what I need to say. I always try to speak in a calm voice and try to simply point out the reality of the situation. The rent is due and must be paid. If it's not paid, I will be forced to take action. The result will all be to the detriment of the tenants.

I point out that they don't want their credit hurt any more than I want to hurt it. They don't want the hassle and costs of an eviction trailing after them anymore than I do. Therefore the best solution is simply to pay the rent, immediately.

Keep in mind that most tenants have access to money from somewhere in order to pay the rent. They may have it in savings that they don't want to touch. Or they may be able to borrow it from relatives. If they now realize that the rent simply *must* be paid, they can usually get it.

Trap

Sometimes tenants need to know that the rent is a high-priority item. Faced with lots of bills, they may decide that one month they'll put the rent down at the bottom of the list. Unless you strongly inform them that they must pay or face the possibility of a bad mark on their credit and even eviction, they may procrastinate. If you're not determined in your approach, you lose.

Determining If the Problem Is
Temporary or Permanent

During your meeting with the tenant when you demand your rent, you must also determine why the tenant isn't paying. Thus far we've been assuming that the tenant can pay, but for whatever reason, won't.

Sometimes, however, it's a far different situation. Perhaps the tenant has been laid off work or has become ill and can't work. Perhaps the tenant has used up all available resources in paying previous months' rents and simply can't pay now. What do you do now?

My feeling is you must decide whether the situation is hopeless or fixable. Let's take each alternative separately.

A fixable situation is one in which the tenant can't pay now, but has every chance of being able to pay soon. For example, the tenant may be experiencing a temporary layoff, but the employer has indicated that rehiring will begin in a few weeks. You have to decide if the possibility of his being rehired and then being able to pay the rent is realistic.

Trap

Almost invariably, tenants will say that they have money coming in soon. Putting off the landlord has gotten to be one of the most widely played games in the world.

This is not to say that most tenants do this insincerely. Many actually do believe that the problem is very temporary, and in just a few days it will be solved. You have to determine just how realistic are their expectations.

If it appears that the delay in sending in the rent is temporary, the tenant hasn't been late before, and is keeping up the property, then you may want to wait. How *long* to wait is a matter for your good judgment.

Trap

The longer you wait, the lower your leverage. Presumably you have at least a month's rent in a security/cleaning deposit. If you wait two weeks, you now only have two weeks of security/cleaning deposit left. If you wait a month, it's all gone. If the tenants now leave and the place is a mess, you have no money in reserve to use for cleanup. (You already took it out for the month's rent.)

My own feeling is that it's important to have a heart-to-heart talk with the tenants, in which you help them to see the reality of the situation. You need to emphasize that the longer they stay without paying, the more rent becomes due. If they can't pay this month it's going to be doubly hard to pay the next, and triply hard to pay the third.

You need to reemphasize that if they don't pay they will jeopardize their credit, and that in today's world good credit is more valuable than gold. Also, you won't be able to give the next landlord a good recommendation.

Finally, you need to spell out the eviction procedure in your state. You need to point out that they will be responsible for eviction costs, and that if they don't pay or vacate, they may ultimately be tossed out onto the street.

Tip

Keep your eye on your goal. You want the tenant to pay the rent or to leave. You're not interested in keeping a tenant who doesn't pay. Don't make the mistake of waving a long-term rental agreement in the tenant's face and saying that they are committed for the next nine months (or whatever) to pay the rent. You're far better off to have a tenant out who doesn't pay, than to have them in.

Most tenants will comply one way or another. They will either pay or make arrangements to leave. If they plan to leave, be sure to emphasize that they need to pay for the days they actually stay there.

Tenants Who Want to Make Partial Payments

Often when tenants can't pay the rent in full they want to make partial payments. You have to be careful about accepting these.

If the tenants are likely to be able to continue to make rent payments (they're experiencing is a temporary setback), then you may want to accept partial payments, say payments made every week, until they are able to pay a full month in advance.

On the other hand if the tenants have problems that are permanent in nature, and are unlikely to be able to continue to make payments, accepting a partial payment may simply delay the inevitable.

Trap

In all states there are set procedures for eviction. In California, for example, a landlord must first give a tenant a three-day "Notice To Quit Or Pay." The landlord must then file an Unlawful Detainer Action with the court. This is a priority case, and usually you will get a speedy hearing and the court will order an eviction within a few weeks.

If, however, you accept a partial rent payment after the three-day notice and before eviction, you may have to start the four-to-six-week process all over again from scratch. Paying one week's rent, in effect, can buy the shrewd tenant another's month's delay. Check with an eviction attorney for the rules in your area.

Eviction proceedings usually move forward smoothly, as long as the tenant doesn't contest them. Tenants almost never do, since, after all, they are behind in rent and what can they say?

However, sometimes tenants will contest. Perhaps they haven't paid the rent because there is some physical problem with the property, such as a drain or appliance that doesn't work and that you haven't fixed. Or perhaps the tenant claims that he or she is too ill to move.

In this case the judge may postpone the hearing, or may even delay or refuse to grant an Unlawful Detainer Action. In that case you've got a nonpaying tenant staying in your property. (See the movie *The Presidio* for the worst possible form of this scenario!)

However, if you've done your homework, you will know in advance why the tenant hasn't paid the rent. You will have corrected any physical problems with the property, determined if there are any other extenuating circumstances such as illness, and gotten other medical opinion or made special arrangements with the tenant. (It's rare today that someone can't be moved for medical reasons.)

Tenants Who Leave the Place a Mess

After decades in the real estate rental business, I've come to the conclusion that cleanliness is *not* next to godliness. It is strictly a matter of personal opinion. A plate that one person is willing to eat off would make another person throw up. Similarly, when it comes to rentals, the landlord's idea of what is clean often differs dramatically from the tenant's. This always comes to the fore when tenants leave the property. Invariably there's a difference of opinion between the tenants and the landlord. I can't think of the number of times I've walked into a place that I considered completely filthy only to have the tenants turn to me with great sincerity and say, "But it's cleaner than when we moved in!" Note: This is not to say that tenants always leave rentals dirty. I have had tenants who did indeed leave the property cleaner than when they moved in. In the case of one rather expensive property, I was very concerned about the tenants because they had five children and several pets. So I was holding a security/cleaning deposit of $2,500.

When they moved out, the place was so clean that I returned all of it to them except for $20, which I paid to a trash service to haul away some garbage bags they had left at the curb. Unfortunately, in the case of cleanliness they tended to be the exception rather than the rule.

Trap

Be aware that you can't require a tenant to leave a place *exactly* as they found it. During the course of tenancy there is always "reasonable wear and tear" that will occur. Tenants cannot be charged for this. They can be charged only for *un*reasonable wear and tear, over and above what might normally be expected for such a rental.

Given the opportunity for disagreement over what constitutes clean and dirty, particularly when the tenants leave and want their deposit back, I think it's always a good idea to use the method of a before-and-after "walk-through."

The Walk-Through

In a walk-through, before the tenants move in (but after paying the rent and the security/cleaning deposit and signing the contract), you walk through the rental with a checklist. Both you and the tenants should carefully note any existing wear, damage, or dirt to the premises. You should also note where the premises are clean, newly painted, or newly carpeted. Then, after going through the entire rental, both you and the tenants sign the walk-through sheet. This then becomes the basis for determining any unreasonable wear and tear the tenants have put on the premises when they move out.

Trap

If it ever gets to court (usually small-claims), the burden of proving that the property was clean and the tenants made it dirty is usually on you, the landlord. Therefore you want to be very careful with the walk-throughs.

Tip

Sometimes tenants will dispute even what they've signed on the walk-through. Therefore, if I'm suspicious that this might happen, I take color photographs of the premises prior to the tenants moving in. I have even videotaped rentals using a camcorder!

If, however, you use photos or videotape, be absolutely sure that you are able to identify the date the shots were taken. Including a portion of a dated newspaper can help, as can having a third party, perhaps a neighbor, walk through with you and appear in the photos or tape.

Later, *after* the tenants have moved all of their things out, you can walk through with them again and compare the original checklist with the one you now make. Hopefully, when confronted with the written evidence, the tenants who have made a mess or left the premises dirty will fess up, and not complain about your withholding a portion of the security/cleaning deposit to pay for it. If there's still disagreement, bringing out the photos or videotape will usually put an end to that.

Trap

Be careful of how you describe the premises on your initial walk-through. If you describe a wall, for example, as having a few marks on it, later on when you get the property back and find the wall scuffed, dirty, and with holes in it, be prepared for a tenant to say something like, "See, it was marked when I rented it. It says so right there on the sheet."

You're better off to originally write something such as, "three small scuff marks on surface of wall, none larger than two inches." The more detailed you are, the better off you'll be on the second walk-through.

Tip

In the initial walk-through, it's probably a good idea for you, the landlord, to be as positive about the property as possible. Yes, you certainly want to note anything that's broken, damaged, or dirty. But keep in mind that every time you mark something down, you open yourself up to the tenants later on asserting that what was in fact something quite small, was something quite large.

The After-Rental Walk-Through

The initial walk-through is usually quite easy. The tenants will often be as anxious to point out any defects as you are to say the place looks great. Since it's the beginning of the rental, and both of you want to be on your best behavior for the other, it's easy to compromise and come up with an agreement on a description for almost everything. Then both of you, feeling good about what you've done, will sign the agreement and the tenant will move in.

The after-rental walk-through, however, is quite different. Here, the tenants are likely going to be very defensive. They are focusing on getting back that cleaning/security deposit, and they may try to minimize any problems.

The best way of handling this, I believe, is to try to be as reasonable as possible. If you made detailed descriptions when you moved in (preferably with photos), you shouldn't have too much trouble. You can usually appeal to the tenants' sense of fair play.

The second walk-through is also usually a compromise. In it, you are often forced by the tenant to compromise. You may realize that you'll have to repaint a bedroom because of the marks on the walls. You'd sorely love to take the costs out of the tenants' deposit. However, the tenant points out that it was somewhat soiled before you rented it, and that the existing marks are just normal wear and tear. You're forced to grit your teeth and admit that it's true. You see money flying out the window.

The advantage of the second walk-through is that everything gets out in the open. The tenants get to express themselves, as do you, and what you end up with, finally, is an agreement over how much, if any, of the rental deposit to withhold. When you both sign off, you know that there are not going to be any hard feelings, or any lawsuits, later on.

Trap

Some tenants will stonewall the final walk-through. A wall will be dirty; they will say it's clean. A stove will be caked with grease; they will say it was that way when they moved in, even though the initial walk-through shows it clean.

A timid landlord, one who can easily be intimidated, is often put off by this sort of performance. Expecting the tenants to be cooperative and instead finding them saying black is white, may throw such a landlord off his stride. The result may be that he or she concedes a whole lot to the tenant that really isn't true.

When confronted by such a tenant, I simply will say that I disagree with them, my original walk-through sheet reflects that I am right, and I am going to deduct appropriately. (Having photos, videotape, or another witness available to back me up certainly helps.) In other words, I stonewall right back. Faced with the reality of the situation, tenants will usually begin to be more accepting and willing to compromise.

Not Having the Tenant Walk-Through

There is usually no requirement that you and the tenant do the final walk-through together. I recommend it, because it avoids misunderstandings and complications later on.

However, some landlords, aware of how difficult a second walk-through is, may try to put the tenants off and do it after they leave.

This is a mistake. If the tenants insist on being there for the final walk-through and you don't allow them to be, they can use this against you later on in a small-claims action to reclaim their security/cleaning deposit. It's better to bite the bullet and do the walk-through with the tenant than to hide your head in the sand and avoid it.

Trap

Sometimes, after the final walk-through has revealed all sorts of problems, the tenant will want an opportunity to reclean and fix up the place. In other words, they agree with you that there are problems, they just want the opportunity to correct them.

My feeling is that unless there is a pressing time reason why you can't do this, you should offer them the opportunity. Give them another day, for example, to go back and clean up further. (There may even be a statutory requirement in your area that you do this.)

Tip

My own experience is that allowing the tenants to go back and try again on the cleaning is almost always a waste of time, unless it's some small specific thing that needs correction. If they didn't see the dirt the first time, they probably won't see it the second, either.

The Tenant Who Sues for Return
of the Cleaning/Security Deposit

You should be aware that a tenant can always haul you into court and sue you for return of the cleaning/security deposit. Since such action is usually in small-claims court, it may not cost the tenant anything more than some time. On the other hand time may be very precious to you, and fighting a court action over a few hundreds dollars may simply not be worthwhile.

As a result, you may want to settle even if you feel you are 100 percent in the right. Simply giving the tenant a few nuisance bucks to drop the action and sign a release may be worthwhile.

On the other hand, if you feel you were totally justified in withholding a portion or all of the security/cleaning deposit, and if you have the documentation to back you up as well as the time to pursue it, by all means do so. There's no reason a landlord should be taken to the cleaners by a conniving tenant.

8

Maintenance Minefields

When you buy an investment house you always have choices. Usually the decision is based on financial attractiveness. However, it would be a mistake to make your purchase based solely on finances. There are other critical elements to the purchase decision. In this chapter we'll consider one of the most important, future maintenance costs and problems. (See also the section on maintenance in Chapter 5.)

When you purchase an investment home you buy not only the property but any physical headaches that may go with it. These can potentially use up enormous time, money, and effort and, in some cases, make the ownership of the property a horrible experience. (I know. I recently sold a property that was a maintenance nightmare. Though I made a profit on the sale, I celebrated just at being rid of it.)

Most investors new to real estate tend to minimize the potential maintenance costs of operating a problem property. This is usually a big mistake, because it changes the whole cashflow equation. Without considering maintenance, a property may show a positive cashflow. With maintenance, it may be a negative.

The mistake is to consider only "PITI" when you purchase. (As experienced investors know, PITI stands for Principle, Interest, Taxes, and Insurance, the fixed costs that you'll have to pay each month.) For example, you may be purchasing a rental house where the PITI is $750 a month. After checking out other rentals in the area, you are pretty sure you can rent the property for $800 a month. That gives you a cashflow cushion of $50 a month.

However, when you buy the property, you find that your maintenance costs, over a period of a year or two, are actually running you

$125 a month. Thus, instead of a positive $50, you have a negative $75 that you must pay out of your pocket each month.

You don't believe a rental could have a $125 maintenance cost a month? Think again. In any given month your total costs may be zero, but when you average them out over a couple of years, $125 is probably a very low monthly figure for many rental homes. Keep that in mind when you are considering your investment property purchase.

Trap

Don't underestimate the psychological effect of a negative cashflow, even a small one, resulting from maintenance problems. A "good" rental for most landlords is one they don't have to think about. It takes care of itself and doesn't require time, effort, or money.

A "bad" rental, on the other hand, is one in which you get called to fix something every month. You begin to dread the call. You find you are swearing at the property. Soon, even though in the long run the property may end up making you a healthy profit, you are eager to dump it just to get rid of the headache.

Eventually you may sell too soon or too cheaply, just to get out from under a maintenance-heavy property. As noted, don't underestimate the psychological drain of maintenance. It can literally turn a good property into a bad one.

Tip

Remember, as noted earlier, that older properties always have more maintenance costs than newer ones. If you have a choice, buy a newer investment property, preferably one that's 15 years old or less.

The following are some of the maintenance problems you may run into. Keep in mind, of course, that these problems won't necessarily crop up. It's just that if you are watching out for them, you can be doubly sure to avoid them. (Also check into Chapter 4.)

Houses with Serious Defects

Many times a house with a serious defect is an investor's opportunity. The serious defect, such as a cracked foundation, a bad roof, soil slippage, can result in a much lower price. If you can go in and correct the problem, often you can resell at a hefty profit.

The trouble is that sometimes the problem can only be stabilized, not corrected. And in the process it can turn into a maintenance horror.

For example, a friend of mine recently bought a house with a large swimming pool. The pool was empty, and showed evidence of cracks. Because of this, the seller discounted the price. My friend bought the house intending to fix the pool and resell for a profit.

The trouble was that the pool was very old and very resistant to being fixed. It turned out that the cracks were mainly superficial, which was a relief. Dealing with "through-the-wall" pool cracks can be very expensive.

However, the plaster was old and dilapidated. Rather than replaster the pool (a very expensive proposition), my friend repainted it for under $500. Then he filled it, and his problems really began.

The plumbing for the pool was corroded, which meant that it continually leaked water. To fix the plumbing meant digging up the concrete around the pool. Again at great cost. So he just kept refilling it with water.

Adding large amounts of new water, however, diluted the chlorine stabilizer and resulted in the pool's needing more chlorine. Before he realized it, the pool was out of chlorine and soon was filled with yellow-and-black algae. Further, the algae burrowed behind the new paint and into the plaster, making it almost impossible to remove. Soon my friend was dumping huge amounts of chlorine into the pool just to keep the water blue and clean for the tenants.

In short, the costs of just maintaining the pool's chemicals soon came to better than $100 a month. Add to that water, plus pool service (for cleaning), and the costs were over $200 a month. But what was worse, my friend had to be there every week when the tenants called to complain that the pool just wasn't clean. The combination of cost, effort, and time spent had turned the pool into a maintenance nightmare.

I'm not suggesting that every pool will be this bad. I am pointing out, however, that maintenance costs can arise out of a serious defect that you hope to correct but may be unable to completely fix.

Tip

The serious defect problems that are most likely to become maintenance headaches are:

Leaky pools

Leaky roofs

Uneven floors caused by a broken or bad foundation

Recurring cracks in walls and ceilings

Old Plumbing Problems

Another area to be concerned about when you purchase is old plumbing. If the investment house you are looking at is 25 years or older, this is something you should seriously look at. It may be that the potential costs of maintaining the old plumbing will deter you from purchasing!

Today, in most states, house plumbing is all copper, although in some areas PVC pipe is used. Both are excellent when it comes to durability and longevity.

However, 25 years ago the water plumbing of choice in most areas (and still in some) was galvanized pipe. This is essentially steel pipe that has been galvanized to slow rusting. The pipe, however, always rusts through eventually.

I have found two big problems with old houses containing galvanized pipe. First, in some areas the pipe, which comes underground to the house, can react electrically with the ground. (The electrical systems of most houses are grounded through the cold water pipes.) This produces electrolysis, which over the years thins the pipe, allows rusting, and produces leaks. Since the pipes are often located in ceilings and walls, these leaks can suddenly burst forth, flooding whole areas of the house. This is particularly the case if the leak occurs when the tenant isn't at home and there isn't anyone available to turn off the water. (I've seen water pouring out of the doors of a home where a leak had gone undetected for several days.)

Insurance will usually cover the damage to the property, at least for the first occurrence, but typically will not cover the cost of repairing the leak!

Trap

Your insurance usually will *not* cover the cost of damage by water leaks to tenants' furniture and possessions. For that kind of coverage, the tenants must carry their own insurance. However, if they don't, they may turn around and sue you for damage caused by your leaking pipes. Therefore, it's best to use preventative care on such pipes whenever possible.

Tip

For correcting accessible leaks in galvanized pipe, most hardware stores sell pressure clamps. You simply apply these around the leak and tighten the screws. They usually work well only as a temporary fix.

Another problem with old galvanized pipe can arise from the fact that the pipe in some cases is buried in the ground under the house. This is particularly true with older homes that have slabs.

The old pipe can rust out and turn into something resembling Swiss cheese, with holes and leaks everywhere. The trouble is that, in order to correct a leak, you have to break through the slab. This means ripping up the flooring and using a jackhammer to get through the cement just to get to the problem pipe. Then you need to cement in a slab repair and replace the flooring. An expensive and time-consuming job.

The final answer to the problem of galvanized pipe is to replace it all with modern copper plumbing. However, be aware that the cost of doing this can be around $5,000 for an average-sized house. Further, it usually involves ripping holes in walls and ceilings, and most tenants will object to the inconvenience while they are living there.

Tip

One solution is to offer the tenants a week's free rent while the plumbing work is going on. That usually keeps them happy and cooperative. You don't lose a tenant, and you haven't spent a great deal of money.

There's another unrelated problem involving old plumbing, and this has to do with drain lines. (Before we were talking about water lines, the kind that bring hot and cold water to your faucet. Now we're talking about drains, which take the water away to a sewer or septic tank.)

Houses with very old drains tend not to have too many problems here. These very old homes (more than 35 years old) often have cast-iron drains that connect together with hemp and lead. They can last almost forever, providing they aren't disturbed.

However, houses built between 25 and 35 years ago often used a drain made out of a material resembling compressed tar paper. These are the houses that can present real maintenance headaches today. (Younger houses almost universally use a kind of black PVC pipe that also will last almost forever.)

The houses with the tar paper drains (we're speaking here of the lines leading from the house to the sewer or septic system) often leak, and attract the roots of trees and plants. These roots get in the lines, then break and clog them.

This sort of problem means that you will get frequent calls from the tenants complaining about clogged drains. You'll call out the plumber, who will use a long metal snake to root out the line, and the problem will be solved—for a few months, until the roots grow back. You can find yourself spending a hundred dollars or so every few months on this problem.

Tip

You can buy chemicals to add to the toilet that will discourage root growth. My experience, however, is that tenants don't bother to do this.

The worst scenario is when the roots break, or clog a pipe to the point where it can't be rooted out. Instead it must be replaced. Then it gets very costly.

The last time I had a sewer pipe replaced it cost $1,200. And that was just to go about 20 feet from the house to the street!

Septic Systems

Finally, septic systems can cause serious maintenance headaches. When the sewer line from a house does not connect to a public sanitary sewer line, but instead goes to a holding tank somewhere on the property, that's a septic system. The holding tank takes care of solid waste. Liquid waste then usually drains to a leach field, where it percolates harmlessly into the ground.

The trouble is that a septic tank must be pumped out every four to five years. (There are septic service companies you can find in the phone book that do this.) If it's not done, the solid waste will rise and eventually travel with the liquid waste to the leach field, plugging it. When that happens, sewer water rises to the surface, producing a bad odor and causing an unsanitary situation. The only solution is to replace the leach field, and that usually costs thousands of dollars.

Trap

Sometimes you can't replace a leach field! Each county usually has a sanitarian whose job it is to come out and determine where a leach field will go. Leach fields require a lot of room. However, some properties are simply too small to have a secondary leach field. In that case the sanitarian may condemn your property! You won't be able to rent it or have anyone live in it until you can provide a sanitary sewer system. Your only solution may be to hook up to a public sewer, if one is available, or to negotiate with neighbors for the use of their land for your leach field.

All in all, old plumbing problems can cause some of the most serious rental house maintenance problems. You can easily avoid most of them, however, by buying a new property. If, however, you do decide to buy an older home, it will be well worth your while to check out the plumbing system beforehand.

Old Electrical Problems

Before buying an old investment house, you should also consider potential electrical maintenance problems. This applies usually to houses more than 30 years old.

Aluminum Wiring

The problems are usually of three kinds. The most widely known of these is caused by aluminum wiring.

About 20 years ago, many houses were wired using less expensive aluminum wire instead of copper. There's nothing wrong with aluminum wiring, except that if it isn't attached properly to terminals, it can actually unwind and cause shorts, which can result in fires. If you buy a home with aluminum wiring, you may find that at some point you will be required to retrofit, either by completely rewiring with copper or by replacing terminals with approved connectors. Either way, it can be very expensive.

Tip

If the investment house you are considering has aluminum wiring, check to see if it has already been retrofitted. If not, look into the possibility of having the seller do it as a condition of sale.

If you are buying an older home, say one that is 40 years old or older, you may have a different kind of electrical problem. The house may indeed be wired with copper. But instead of circuit breakers, which are now commonly used, the house may have fuses. And the insulation on the wiring, which today is plastic, may be a mixture of cloth strands and tar, which can deteriorate over time.

It may turn out that fuse boxes, lights, switches, and plugs short out. This could mean that every month you (or an electrician) will be at the house, fixing some other circuit.

What's worse, if the wiring really deteriorates, you may have to completely rewire. The last price I heard for rewiring a house was upwards of $7,500.

Finally, the last maintenance problem that you might run into with wiring, in houses that are 35 or more years old, is the lack of a ground wire. All modern homes carry three electrical wires to every outlet and most switches and lights. Perhaps you've seen them. There's a white neutral wire, which carriers the electricity back to the main circuit box; a black wire, which is "hot" and carries electricity to the plugs; and a ground wire, which typically has no insulation, or if it does, is usually green.

In older houses this third wire, the uninsulated or green one, is sometimes absent. What that means is that there is no grounding at a plug.

Some older houses have no ground wire at all. No plugs, switches, lights, or appliance connections are grounded.

It might be argued that if the house has lasted for 40 or more years without grounds, what's the problem?

The problem has to do with safety. A tenant using an ungrounded plug, particularly in the bathroom or the kitchen where the floor might be wet, could be electrocuted. You certainly wouldn't want to be liable for that.

Thus, if you purchase a house without ground wires, you may find that over time you are adding them to the bathrooms, the kitchen, and even other rooms in the house. The cost is virtually the same as for rewiring. It's very expensive.

Tip

It's easy to tell if a house lacks a ground wire. If the receptacles are old and have only two holes instead of the usual three, it's almost a sure bet. If there are three holes, you can use an inexpensive electrical ground-checker, bought at Radio Shack, to tell you if the center hole is grounded. Simply check all the plugs in the house.

Earthquake Refitting

In areas where earthquakes are common (particularly the west coast), new laws are on the way that may require you, as the owner of a house, to retrofit that house to prevent serious damage during an earthquake. Typically, the laws are being written to say that you can't resell without the retrofit.

The problem is that these laws in most areas are not yet on the books. That means that if you buy an older investment home today, by the time you're ready to resell you may have to bear the full cost of earthquake retrofitting!

Since this probably will run you from $3,500 to $10,000 a house, it's a big consideration. While technically it may not be a maintenance cost, it is a cost.

Tip

If the house you are purchasing is more than 15 years old, be sure to get an earthquake safety check done on it before you buy. If the house is not seismically safe, you may want to pass, or condition the sale on the current seller's correcting the problem.

Large Yards and Large Lawns

As already noted in earlier chapters, most landlords expect the tenants to take care of the rental premises in a single-family dwelling. That includes mowing and caring for the yard and garden. You will probably expect this when you buy a rental home.

This usually works out as planned, as long as the yard and lawn are small. Tenants typically will take good care of small areas.

However, if you buy a rental home that has a large yard and lawn, you may have a problem. Most tenants balk at the prospect of spending their weekends taking care of your yard. Thus when you drive by you may see long, unkempt grass and lots of weeds and shrubs that have a wild, disheveled look. Soon the neighbors are complaining, and perhaps you get a letter from the homeowners' association or the city demanding that you clean up. What's worse, once the tenants have moved, the yard may be so run-down that it will look bad even after it's been trimmed, making it hard to rerent the house.

But, you point out to the tenants, they agreed in the rental agreement to take care of the property maintenance. They'll nod and say, "It's more than we bargained for. Get a gardener."

You may rant and storm. You may even threaten to raise their rent to compensate for getting a gardener (in which case they will threaten to move). But in the end, a gardener you will get. And this will cost you anywhere from $50 on up, each month, in additional maintenance.

Tip

Don't be suckered into lowering a tenant's rent on the promise that he or she will take care of a very large yard. Maybe it will be cared for during the first months, but almost invariably the tenant will realize that the small reduction in rent isn't worth the large effort in gardening. The tenant may say, "Raise the rent back up to normal and get a gardener."

Trap

Tenants also won't want to pay for the water to properly take care of a large yard. Therefore, many landlords pay for the water themselves. This is an additional maintenance cost. Usually it's fairly inexpensive. However, in arid areas it can be quite costly.

My suggestion is that when you are considering the purchase of an investment home, you go for houses that have small yards, small gardens, and small lawns. The maintenance headaches you'll avoid and the cost you'll save makes this very worthwhile.

Swimming Pools and Spas

We have already touched on swimming pools at the beginning of this chapter and elsewhere. But here, let's talk about a *working* spa or pool, one with no problem.

My experience has been that you will need to hire a maintenance service. In general, you can't count on tenants to take care of a pool or spa. Since it's not their own, they tend to overlook the adding of chemicals and the cleaning.

A pool/spa service costs anywhere from $35 a month on up. Plan on paying for it if you have a pool or spa.

Trap

Sometimes tenants will say that they will take care of the pool or spa if you will provide the chemicals and reduce the rent slightly, say $20 or $30 a month.

You may think this is a good deal, but beware. In my experience they still won't do the job, they just won't complain about it to you. Then when they eventually move out you may be stuck with a pool or spa that has been ruined by algae.

Asphalt Driveways

I have nothing against asphalt driveways. (I do, however, think they don't show as well as cement driveways.)

However, the problem is that they are subject to breaking as tree roots pop through. Further, winter rains and snows can take the surface off them fairly quickly.

Thus, if you purchase a rental home with an asphalt driveway, be prepared to have it resurfaced every spring, usually at a cost of around $100. And also be prepared to have it replaced every 7 to 10 years, usually at a cost of several thousands of dollars.

If you have a choice between a house with a cement driveway and another with asphalt, I'd take the cement every time.

Trap

Beware of heavily cracked cement driveways. They can cost more to replace than those made of asphalt!

Old Central Air Conditioners

If you live in a hot climate (the south or southwest), chances are the investment home you are purchasing has an air conditioner. That could be a maintenance problem later on, if the air conditioner is old.

Air conditioners normally don't require service. However, as they age problems can occur. Occasionally one of the lines will spring a leak, and you may need to have someone come out and add coolant. A blower motor may die and need to be replaced. Or the worst could happen, the condenser could fail.

If you purchase a house with an old air conditioner, all of these maintenance problems may happen to you over a period of a couple of years, perhaps costing you several thousands of dollars.

Tip

When you purchase an older home, have the sellers buy a home warranty policy for you. It should cover the air conditioner for at least a year, and if anything fails during that period, the warranty organization should pay for it, less a small deductible.

Garbage Disposers

I know of no household appliance that causes more trouble than garbage disposers. It seems they are forever getting jammed, requiring that either you or a plumber get out to the house and fix them. Or the motor burns out, requiring that you replace them. Or they spring a leak that may or may not be fixable, meaning, in the latter case, that you will have to replace them.

Tip

The most common problem with a garbage disposer is that it gets jammed. This usually occurs because too much material is shoved down it all at once.

If you have to respond to every jammed garbage disposer incident, you will spend a good bit of your life at your rental, getting the thing to work again and again. Therefore, when a tenant moves in, I always explain how the disposer works. I show the tenant the reset button and leave a hex key that can be used to unjam the unit. Usually tenants are happy to do it themselves, since it's a simple task, and get the unit running right away, rather than call and wait a day for you to respond.

If your rental house has a garbage disposer, plan on at least one maintenance call every six months. There may be more or less, depending on how lucky you are.

Tip

Often, the first time a garbage disposer goes out in a rental unit, I replace it with a new, more expensive unit, with at least one-half horsepower. A bigger unit costs only a few dollars more than a smaller one. Yet it will jam far less frequently. And after all, the major cost is in the labor required for replacement, not the unit itself.

Paint

Most new investors, when buying a rental home, discount the paint. Usually the house has recently been painted to get it ready for the sale. If it's a fixer-upper, then the cost of having you paint it up is usually figured into the price.

However, there are hidden maintenance costs in painting. Each time you turn over a tenant, chances are you will need to repaint some portion of the house. If you replace tenants annually, then you've got several hundreds of dollars in annual painting costs to consider. If you replace tenants more often, you'll have higher costs. Less often, and you'll have lesser costs.

Tip

Don't think that because a tenant stays on for years, you won't have to repaint. Every few years you will want to come in and repaint, just to keep the tenant happy. A long-term, good-paying tenant is an asset you don't want to lose.

Trap

Don't think you can take the cost of repainting from a tenant's security/cleaning deposit. That deposit covers "cleaning," not painting. Unless the tenant did damage that can only be covered by paint, you will find that in most cases local or state ordinances will not allow you to take the costs of repainting out of a cleaning deposit. (Remember, a tenant is allowed "reasonable wear and tear.")

Carpeting

The trouble with carpeting is that almost all tenants want it, but very few are willing to keep it really clean.

Today most rentals have wall-to-wall carpeting. (Some of course have wood floors and area rugs, but it's hard to find a rental without carpeting of some sort.) In order to keep that carpeting in good shape, it must be vacuumed regularly and shampooed every so often. Most importantly, care must be taken not to allow stains onto it.

Unfortunately, in my experience tenants tend to be less careful with carpeting than homeowners. What this means is that when you get your property back after a tenant moves out, you will very likely need to do some work on the carpets. At the least this will include vacuuming and shampooing. At the worst, it will mean ripping up the carpets because they have been badly stained, and replacing them.

Hopefully most of the cleaning cost will come from the security/cleaning deposit. But probably not all of it will. You will undoubtedly end up footing a part of the bill yourself.

Most homeowners replace carpeting every 7 to 10 years. Most landlords, however, replace it every 3 to 5 years. It's for this reason that landlords tend to seek out inexpensive, yet attractive and long-wearing carpeting.

It's important to realize up front, when you purchase a rental property, that carpeting is going to be one of your regular big expenses. No, you may not have to pay anything in maintenance for carpeting in a given year. But, over a five-year period, you will surely end up paying a significant amount.

Trap

When you are making a purchase decision on a rental unit, don't make the mistake of plotting out the maintenance costs just for a single year. Some years may have far higher costs than others. Try doing it on a three- to five-year projection. (See the time line in Chapter 4.)

Tip

You don't have to pay an arm and a leg for carpeting. What you want is a strong, attractive carpet, usually nylon, that doesn't show dirt and that isn't expensive. Try calling local property management companies. Often they can give you the names of carpet brokers in your area. These people sell carpeting almost exclusively to commercial and large residential buyers, for about half of what the retail stores charge. Almost always they will be happy to sell to you, if you buy a whole house or apartment's worth. They also can normally arrange for installation.

Appliances, Including Refrigerators

Almost all rental units come with some appliances. These can include the following:

Oven

Range

Garbage Disposer

Dishwasheroe

Refrigerator

Washer

Dryer

Compactor

All appliances can be headaches. Over the course of a year or two one or more is likely to go down, requiring that either you, or a service person, repair it.

The most common problem is with garbage disposers, as noted earlier. However, other common problems include broken elements in electric ranges and ovens, broken dishwasher pumps and timers, refrigerators that stop cooling, washers whose motors give out, dryers with broken belts, and compactors that won't compact.

Trap

Beware of replacing the heating elements in ranges and ovens. Often the cost of two elements is as much as for the replacing of the entire unit! If it's an old appliance, it might be better to replace it than to fix it.

Tip

Smart landlords limit the number of appliances in a unit. In inexpensive units, I have seen landlords remove garbage disposers and dishwashers and not replace them. The idea was that they could rent the property without them and thus save a lot of money on maintenance costs. In more expensive units, however, tenants expect garbage disposer and dishwashers, and you'll just have to bear the brunt of the maintenance costs.

Most tenants do not expect a refrigerator, washer, dryer, or compactor (the compactor may be expected in a luxury unit). My suggestion is that you do not supply these in your rental. By not doing so, you'll save a lot of headaches.

On the other hand, if you do supply them, I suggest you make it clear that you will not be responsible if they break down. For example, a friend who has rentals supplied a refrigerator, washer, and dryer. (They came with the house when he bought it.) However, he told the tenants that if and when the units broke, he would not fix them. Rather, it would be up to the tenants to replace them with their own. It worked out quite well. During the first year of tenancy, both the refrigerator and the clothes dryer broke down. The tenants got rid of them and bought their own. It's been three years, and the clothes washer is still working. Either way, these appliances haven't cost my friend a dime in maintenance.

Furniture

Normally a landlord does not supply furniture for a house, condo, or other unit. The exception is when it is a short-term rental such as a vacation property. For example, I know an agent who has a house on a lake in California's Sierra mountains. The house rents for a thousand dollars a week during the three months of summer. The rest of the year it can't be rented at all.

Consequently, she uses it for her vacations nine months of the year and rents it out for three, fully furnished.

Trap

Be careful of the tax laws when it comes to renting a vacation home. If you use the property yourself for more than 14 days out of the year, your ability to deduct depreciation and other expenses may be eliminated or severely limited. See your tax accountant for more information.

When you have a furnished rental, you'll find that you are constantly replacing the furniture. It gets nicked, stained, or broken. Generally speaking, it is very hard to charge the tenants for the damage, unless they actually broke something and you can pinpoint what it was. Thus the maintenance costs are usually yours to bear. (Of course, if you're getting a high enough rental rate, you can afford to replace furniture!)

The way to reduce maintenance costs is to purchase commercial furniture. This is the kind that you'll find in motels and hotels.

Commercial furniture is marketed under many brands. Generally it is fairly neutral in design and color, yet it stands up to hard use very well over time. It also is relatively inexpensive when compared to furniture that you would buy for your own home.

Check with a local motel/hotel owner to see where they are purchasing their furniture. (Try an independent. You're more likely to get the owner and find him or her willing to talk.) In large cities, commercial furniture dealers advertise as such.

Tip

You may need a "resale license" to purchase from such dealers. A resale license simply means that you're an intermediary and not the ultimate purchaser, hence the dealer doesn't charge you sales tax. A resale license is often used by dealers as a means of keeping the general public away. (They don't want to sell the commercial furniture to the public, because it would cut into sales of the more expensive residential lines.)

Of course, you are the final purchaser. However, you can sometimes overcome the problem if you have a friend with a resale license. He or she can buy the furniture for you, and then you can buy it from your friend, of course then paying the appropriate sales tax. (Don't try to avoid the tax—it will only land both you and your friend in trouble.)

Garage Door Openers

As a final maintenance item, I want to briefly discuss garage door openers.

More expensive properties tend to have garage door openers. They are more or less expected, and you really do need them if you're going to rent out the property to a good tenant. However, these little electrical gadgets can provide a host of troubles.

There are usually three things that go wrong with garage door openers, and sometimes all three are related. The first is that suddenly one day the opener doesn't seem to have enough strength to open the door. The door sticks, half-opened and half-closed.

Of course, the tenants call and you arrive to find everything apparently in working order. Except suddenly the opener isn't strong enough to lift the door.

Usually the reason for the problem is that the track the door runs on has gotten rusty or corroded and is no longer operating smoothly. Usually some silicone-based spray lubricant will solve the problem. If it persists, you may find that your garage door springs have gotten old and no longer rise the way they used to. You should replace them.

Once the door rises smoothly again, you should find that the garage door opener works.

The second problem is often with the remote. Besides batteries going dead, it may simply stop working for a wide variety of reasons. The electronics inside may simply have broken. Or the receiver on the opener may have failed. Or something else could be wrong.

You can try replacing the remote, although this won't help if the problem is in the opener itself.

The last problem arises when the opener unit, the part with the motor, breaks down. It simply doesn't operate anymore.

These can be fixed. I have called the company that manufactured a unit for me and (at no charge!) they sent replacement parts. However, this took several weeks.

Most tenants won't wait several weeks. Therefore my suggestion, when the motor unit doesn't work, is to simply replace the garage door opener. If you buy another unit from the same manufacturer, you may only need to replace the motor unit, keeping the old tracks.

All of which is to say that garage door openers will be a maintenance problem. Expect them to go out about once a year. If it's longer between problems, congratulate yourself on your good luck. If it's less time, well, that's the way it goes. When you buy a house in which there's a garage door opener, I would figure in a maintenance cost of about $5 a month for the unit.

Tip

On a house that isn't a luxury model, consider removing the garage door opener before renting it. Then, when tenants show up, they won't see a garage door opener and won't expect one. You can't do this, however, with luxury units. Tenants paying big rent expect garage door openers, with remotes.

Get It Done Properly

Finally, the best advice of all when it comes to maintenance is, don't wait. When the tenant calls, respond promptly. Tenants figure they are paying you, and if something stops working they aren't getting their full money's worth. It's foolish to lose a tenant over a leaky faucet or cranky garbage disposer.

Unfortunately, many calls come in the evening. Perhaps the tenants have come home from work and suddenly found that something isn't operating. They're mad at it, and take their anger out in a phone call to you.

If you are able, go right over and fix it. Otherwise, tell them it's difficult to fix something at night and, unless it's an emergency (like leaking water or an electrical short), ask them to forbear and explain you'll get to it first thing the next morning. And *do* get to it then.

Don't be like a friend of mine who was the person most ill-suited to being a landlord I have ever met. When a tenant called, no matter what time of the day it was, with a maintenance complaint, he would shout into the phone something such as, "You're living in the house! You fix it!"

That's not something you ever want to tell a tenant, not if you want to keep them paying rent.

Trap

In many states if tenants inform you of a maintenance problem and you refuse to fix it, the tenants may go ahead and fix the problem themselves and then deduct the cost from the rent. You can be sure that if a tenant does this, the cost of repairs is going to be many times what it would have been had you done them.

Don't put off repairs. Get them done quickly.

Tip

On the other hand, some tenants are always calling, often to complain about problems they themselves have caused. Your solution here may be to ask them to leave, then replace them with more reasonable tenants.

9
Home Improvements to Avoid

Sometimes when you are attempting to buy a house for investment, you are offered more than just the house. There may be a pool or a tennis court. There may be a circular driveway or an arbor. There could be a well and pump, or an extra room. In short, you will be told that this particular house has something special that's been added on, that no other house (or few other houses) in the area have—an improvement.

Regardless of what the improvement is, invariably you are asked to pay more for it. You are told the property has increased in value because of the improvement and, therefore, any additional money you pay in price is worthwhile because you'll get it back, and more, when you resell.

But will you really? Do all improvements increase the value of a property? Or do some "improvements" actually *decrease* value?

In this chapter we'll consider homes that have been added to, and how this should affect your investment purchase decision.

The House, the Area, and the Improvement

The general rule is that for an improvement to add value to a property, it must be justified both by the type of house and by the location. By this I mean that if a seller has added a huge family room to a small house in a tract of small houses, chances are the property has been overbuilt. The seller will spend a lot of time trying to get money out of the property that just won't be justified by the neighborhood.

On the other hand, if all the houses in the neighborhood have added a family room, and the prices have risen accordingly, a seller who adds such a room to his house probably is justified in asking for more money.

As a purchaser, the question you must always ask is, does the improvement add real value to the property?

Trap

Don't listen to sellers' arguments on this. Any seller who has added an improvement, or originally paid more for an improvement when the property was purchased, is going to feel that there's added value. Such a seller may point to the additional square footage, and note that at so much a foot, the price has gone up by so many dollars. Or say that, because of the improvement, the property is now worth so much more.

None of this sort of reasoning is valid. A property is worth only what a buyer will pay for it, and that is largely determined by the sale of comparable homes in the area.

Tip

To determine the true value of the property, look at what comparables have sold for. If there are no comparables with a particular improvement, then you have to make your own best guess about how much more someone would be willing to pay for a house that has the improvement. But always try to err on the side of the conservative. Always assume that people will not pay much for an improvement, no matter how much it cost originally.

Bonus Value

The truth of the matter is that most improvements, if they have been done well, are considered bonuses by buyers. A row of oak bookshelves in a den, for example, is probably going to be considered a real plus by buyers. A deck with an overhang in the backyard is likewise going to be considered a bonus. Given a choice between a house with the improvement and one without, most buyers will take the improvement.

Investment Strategy

However, most buyers are not willing to pay extra (or *much* extra) for that improvement. This is critical for you as an investor to understand, because at some point you will be trying to resell that investment property you buy. If you pay extra and then later on find that other buyers won't, you'll lose money.

You must have a very sharp pencil when you purchase an investment property. And in particular you must be very shrewd when it comes to improvements. I'm not saying you should never pay more for a property that's been improved. I'm only saying that you should make your judgment very carefully, or there will come a time when you'll rue the day you paid more.

Having explored the general strategy in theory, let's consider some of the various improvements you're likely to run into. Please keep in mind that the following discussion has to be taken in a general sort of way. I can't know the specific improvement you will be considering. What I am sharing here are my own impressions, based on my own past experiences, of the value added to properties by improvements.

The Pool Home

Does having a swimming pool add value to a property?

Generally the answer is yes, it does. However, the value added is usually in no way commensurate with the cost of the pool.

Today an in-ground swimming pool with equipment and decking, even a modest one, can cost upwards of $25,000. A seller who has spent that amount of money on a pool is going to want to get a lot of the investment back when he or she sells.

The trouble is that, while a pool has a definite bonus value, as discussed above, its value as far as raising the price of the property is minimal. In looking at house *sales* under $200,000, both with and without pools, I rarely see an improvement value for the pool of more than around $5,000.

Further, as the price of the home goes up, in many areas an in-ground pool is expected. Thus it adds no additional value whatsoever.

Trap

Beware of a high-priced home without a pool, in an area where all the other homes have one. Not having a pool in such an area could be a detracting feature and make the house harder to sell.

The Problem Pool

Thus far we've been assuming that the pool is in pristine condition—the water is clear and blue, there are no cracks, the plaster is in good shape, and all of the equipment works. Sometimes, however, that's not the case. Particularly if the pool is old, it can have a host of problems, as we've seen in earlier chapters.

In the worst-case scenario, it is sometimes easier and more financially sound to fill a problem pool with dirt and grow plants in it, than it is to try to fix it and make it swimmable. If you are considering a property with a problem pool, think again. You could be getting into far more trouble than you realize.

Recommendation

My personal recommendation is not to buy a house with a pool, unless it's a high-priced house and all of the homes in the area have pools. If, however, you are determined to go ahead and purchase a pool house, then don't pay much extra for the pool. Just assume it's a bonus. That way when you go to sell, you won't be trying to get extra money out of the property that just isn't there.

The Add-On

People add all sorts of things onto homes. They add extra rooms, garden windows (that are made of glass and metal and extend out from the house), skylights, built-in bookshelves, porches, decks, and on and on. The question is, should you buy a house with such add-ons, and if so, how much more, if anything, should you pay for them?

There are really two questions here. The first has to do with the quality of construction. The question to ask is, was the add-on done in a workmanlike fashion, with a permit from the local building and safety department?

Tip

Never take a seller's word for it that work was done with a permit. It only takes a few minutes of time to go down to the local building department and check it out. Permits are public information. Just give the property address, current owner's name, your interest (prospective buyer), and add-on description. You should be able to quickly find out if the work was done with a permit.

I would never buy a property where a major add-on had been done without a permit. I know that in some locales a lot of work is done by owners "on the side," and properties change hands many times without any problems. But it could just be your luck that when you go to sell, the future purchaser checks it out and discovers the work was done without a permit. That future purchaser demands that the work be brought up to code. Even if you refuse, from then on out you must disclose the lack of permit and that could hinder your sale.

Assuming the work was done properly and with a permit, the next decision to make is whether or not it actually adds true value (as opposed to bonus value) to the property. Here are some *general* rules to follow when you're the prospective purchaser.

Work done inside the property	Adds true value	Doesn't add much value
Bookshelves		X
Kitchen remodeling	X	
Bath remodeling	X	
Closet remodeling		X
Mirrors, new light fixtures		X
New carpeting		X
New paint		X

Work done outside the property	Adds true value	Doesn't add much value
Deck and Overhang		X
Shrubs, flower beds, gardens		X
Add-on room	X	
Separate Garage or room	X	
Fences, walls, ditches, etc.		X

The above list is, of course, abbreviated. There are many more items that could be included. However, I think it gives you an idea. Most things that sellers do don't add value to the property *from your perspective*. Yes, they may cost a lot of money and they make the property more habitable and, as a bonus, they may even make it more salable. But, when you go to buy, if you pay extra for them you could be throwing your money away.

Add-Ons That Add Value

There are, of course, some add-ons that do add value. Generally speaking, when a seller has added on to a kitchen or bath by expanding it, putting in new cabinets, adding new fixtures, and so forth, this directly translates into increased value. Buyers will pay more for homes with improved kitchens and baths. My experience is that they will, in fact, pay double for kitchens, and at least dollar-for-dollar for baths. (For example, if the seller put $3,000 into the kitchen and did it in a workmanlike way, the property is probably worth $6,000 more. If the seller put $3,000 into a bath, the property is probably worth at least $3,000 more. If you pay more when you buy, you should be able to get more when you resell.)

Similarly, room additions that add square footage generally add value. Although here it's a more difficult call. If the addition overbuilds the property, no additional value may accrue. On the other hand, if the house was too small to begin with and the added room now makes it more livable, the increase in value can almost be dollar-for-dollar.

In a like fashion, if the house has no garage, adding one may add value of at least a dollar in value added for a dollar in cost spent. However, a second garage where a usable one is already present may add no value whatsoever. (Sometimes owners will add a second, bigger garage not only to hold cars but to act as a workroom.)

Tip

Check out the addition carefully to make sure it's "legal." Then compare it to other additions in surrounding neighborhoods. Use this "comparable" check to determine if similar additions have added value. If they have, only then be willing to pay more for an add-on.

Added Tennis Court, Basketball Court, or Other Recreational Feature

These add value only if you happen to find someone who is particularly looking for the feature when it comes time for you to resell. For example, a tennis court can cost many thousands of dollars to install (assuming that the property has enough land). However, to a buyer who doesn't play tennis, not only does it not add value, it detracts, because there's less area for that buyer to do what he or she wants. The same holds true for a basketball court or any other recreational feature.

The exception to this, again, is with very high priced property, estate property. In this area, tennis courts may be the norm rather than the exception.

When it comes time for you to purchase for investment a property that has some recreational add-on, you must ask yourself if you're willing to risk waiting to resell until you find a buyer who wants that feature. You must also ask yourself if the house and neighborhood warrant the add-on.

Recommendation

I stay away from such recreational add-ons unless I can get them for virtually nothing added onto the price. If they are only thrown in as bonus value, I figure that's a plus when I resell. However, if I am asked to pay more for them, I decline.

Added Utility Feature

Sometimes properties will have an added utility feature. For instance, the original driveway (which typically leads straight from the street to the garage) may have been added on to so that now there's an additional driveway curving around the front of the house. You can enter, circle around, and come out facing forward. It's a nice feature.

Another utility add-on would be a well. In some parts of the country water is expensive and restricted. Having a legal well means that you can pump directly. While this may not necessarily be used in the house, it could be used to water the yard. If the house has a big yard, this could be another plus.

Other utility add-ons include having 240-volt wiring accessible in the garage; having an extra washbasin installed in the garage; having extra hose bibs in the yard, so that more than the conventional two hoses can be hooked up at once; having sprinklers for the lawn; having a fire-prevention sprinkler system installed; and so forth.

These items are all marvelous bonuses. However, in my opinion they rarely add value to the property when you're considering it for investment. There are, of course, exceptions.

For example, a well in a drought area, where water is severely restricted, could add value. However, be sure the well is "legal."

Trap

Always be sure a well was built with permit, you have the right to pump water from it, and all of the necessary approvals and inspections are up-to-date. In some areas just having a well isn't enough. You also must have the right to the water you pump. Check with a good real estate attorney on this.

Recommendation

I wouldn't pay a dime more for any of the utility features mentioned, with the exception of a well or something similar. There has to be a real need for the feature, before it can increase the price for me.

Above-Ground Spa

I didn't include spas when I discussed pools, because they are usually two different things. (Although some pools come with built-in spas. For those, just reread the section on pools.)

Today, particularly on the west coast, spas (which are like tiny soaking pools, usually three feet deep, with water heated to around 100 degrees) are very common. In the old days, putting in a spa was a major undertaking, involving excavation, building, connecting to gas, plumbing, and electrical lines, and on and on.

Today, spas usually are sold as complete units. You just have them placed on a pad in the yard and connected to your house wiring (permit required), and off you go. Many sellers have installed spas and want extra money for them.

My own feeling is that a spa is the ultimate bonus. It's a wonderful feature, but it does not add monetary value to the property. It does, however, make the property easier to resell.

Recommendation

I never pay extra for a spa that's sold with a property. However, I consider it a prime bonus, and will more seriously consider investing in a house that has one if I plan to resell quickly. If I plan to rent out for an extended period, a spa is out. (Also check into Chapter 8.)

Bottom Line

The variety of items that can be added on to a house is endless. I suppose it's limited only by the imagination of the seller.

In my own experience I have run into room additions that had ceilings less than six feet tall (where I had to duck down in order to get into the room). I've seen bathrooms plumbed between kitchens and garages, where I had to step up to get inside. (They were raised so that the seller could more easily put in the plumbing without digging through the floor of the garage.)

I've seen walls that were crooked, patio covers that were built so flimsily they were ready to fall down, wiring that was substandard, windows that didn't open or close. In short, if you stay in this business long enough, you'll see every kind of add-on imaginable. And you'll quickly come to realize that many of them are done horrendously.

Of course, there's also the other side. There are those additions that are done to code, or even better than code. Add-ons in terms of rooms, kitchen features, bath features, and so forth that truly do add value.

However, my experience overall is that most add-ons simply aren't worth paying an extra penny for. My last bit of advice here is that if you aren't sure whether you should agree to pay the extra bucks that a seller is asking for an add-on, pass. Pass on it, don't buy it. Yes, you might indeed miss a good deal. But chances are that over time you'll do better this way than by paying too much for something that really isn't worth it.

10
Repos and REOs

Thus far we've been assuming you will buy your investment house from a seller who has it listed for sale on the market. Now, however, we're going to take a big step forward and talk about buying an investment property from a lender—a house that has been taken back through foreclosure.

"Foreclosure" can seem a magic word to many investors. It smacks of great prices and opportunities. However, foreclosures are often fraught with problems and pitfalls. Yes, you can make money on them. But if you're not careful, you can lose your shirt as well.

How Foreclosure Works

If you're going to take advantage of it, it's important that you understand how foreclosure works. It's somewhat different state by state, but the process overall is much the same in most areas of the country. There are essentially three stages:

Stage 1. The seller can't or won't make payments, and the lender puts the mortgage in default.

Stage 2. After a period of time determined by each state, the lender "sells" the property to the highest bidder "on the courthouse steps."

Stage 3. Typically the lender is the highest bidder. It takes control of the property and then attempts to resell it as an REO (Real Estate Owned).

You can purchase the property at any stage, often at a much reduced price. But, as noted earlier, you must be wary of the pitfalls.

Stage One—Buying from a Seller in Default

Here the seller can't or won't make payments. He or she is desperate to sell the property, hoping to recoup any equity at the most and save a credit rating at the least. This seller is considered quite motivated, and will be willing to listen to almost any kind of an offer.

When you find someone who is in default, it's now up to you to contact them directly and find out if there is a good deal available. (We'll suggest the best ways to find defaulted mortgages shortly.) Just give this person a call. Explain that you're an investor and that you're looking for property in the area. You heard they were having some difficulty in making payments, and you're wondering if there's a way to make a "win win" situation out of it—they get their credit saved (plus, perhaps, some money, depending on their equity) and you get the property.

Tip

Some people in foreclosure won't want to talk with you. They may be nasty, even offensive. They take their foreclosure personally and may blame everyone but themselves for it. Forget them. They can't be helped, and most likely will lose their house and their credit.

Others will be happy, even eager to talk. Those are the ones you want to work with. When you find such an owner you have to determine what it's going to cost you to take over the property.

What you can offer to the owner is to make up the back payments and penalties and save the owner's credit rating, in exchange for the title to the property. In other words, you can offer to take it over. The advantage here is that you get the property for virtually no money down.

Trap

The downside that many would-be investors overlook is the cost. The existing loan that is in default may not be assumable. You may not only have to make up back payments and penalties, but also secure a new loan with accompanying points and fees. It may cost you many thousands of dollars to take over this property and bail out this owner. You may find that by the time you've added up the costs, it simply isn't worthwhile.

Here is a breakdown of what the costs may be in taking over a property that is in default.

1. Back payments (could be as much as six months of payments or more).

2. Penalties (Each month that the payment is late usually incurs a penalty. There may be additional penalties as time periods in the foreclosure process expire.)

3. New loan costs, including points, fees, title insurance, etc. (Typically this will be about 5 percent of the loan amount—on a $100,000 mortgage, figure about $5,000.)

4. Fixing up the property. The former owner may not have kept the place in great shape once he or she learned they were going to lose it. You may have to spend several thousand in refurbishing and re-landscaping.

It's important that you calculate these costs as accurately as possible *before* you make any kind of offer to the owner. You may find that it simply isn't worth your time to attempt to right the foreclosure and take over the property.

Trap

In the past, some overeager investors have tried to pressure homeowners in default to quickly sign over their properties. These investors, looking to get a "steal," have taken advantage of the fears that frequently hound those who are facing foreclosure. They have offered these people essentially nothing for their homes, even though a substantial equity might be there. Sometimes, just to get out, sellers have sold at a loss of substantial amounts of money.

As a result, many states have enacted laws protecting those in foreclosure from being preyed upon by fortune hunters. Typically such laws allow a certain period of time for recision of a sales agreement when the seller is in default on a mortgage. That period of time can vary from a few days to as long as six months or more.

If you buy from sellers who are in default, be aware that they may come back to haunt you. If the market turns up, they may realize they sold prematurely, and sue to get the property back. You could lose the house as well as a substantial portion of your investment in it. Before you attempt to buy a home from a seller who is in default, check with a good real estate attorney in your state. He or she can give you correct information as to the right of sellers in default to rescind sales.

Buying a house in default can be an excellent way of picking up an investment bargain. Just be sure that you've covered all the bases in terms of costs and sellers' rights.

Where to Find Houses That Are in Default

Agents are a good place to start. Agents will know if any of their sellers is in default. Often they will advertise that fact, indicating that they have a highly motivated seller.

Tip

As an investment buyer, it's a good idea to work with as many brokers as possible. One reason is that only the listing broker may be aware of the default status of a seller. Further, while it is true that most homes that are listed appear on various co-broking services, not all do. Sometimes a broker will hold back a listing that he or she feels is such a bargain that it will sell without being "co-broked." They will keep it for themselves.

Note: Don't worry about agents buying a bargain themselves, before letting you know about it. Nearly all agents depend on commissions from sales for their livelihood. In most cases agents would prefer a sales commission to buying the property themselves.

Individual sellers may also offer their default properties for sale. They may advertise in the paper or even have a FSBO (For Sale By Owner) sign in front.

Check these out. If you can buy directly from the seller without going through an agent, you may end up with a lower price and less of a down payment. (After all, the seller has to pay the agent, and where is that money to come from if not from you?)

Title insurance and escrow companies are also a good source of sellers in default. This is particularly useful in states that use the "trust deed" device instead of the older "mortgage." (Currently over 40 states use the trust deed as the preferred lending device.) In a traditional mortgage there are two parties—the borrower and the lender. With a trust deed, however, there are three parties: the borrower (trustor), the lender (beneficiary), and the trustee. In a trust deed, when the borrower defaults, the lender tells the trustee to begin foreclosure. Since title insurance and escrow companies are often named as trustees, they are often the first to know about defaults.

It's a good idea to make friends with some people in title insurance and escrow companies. They can alert you when there are defaults. (It's public knowledge, just hard to come by.)

Finally, you can read "legal newspapers." The first step in foreclosure is the filing of a notice of default. This notice usually must be filed with the county recorder's office and publicized in a local newspaper. Rather than use the bigger papers, small "legal" newspapers have evolved which carry these notices. A call to any title insurance company officer, or the county clerk's office, should get you the name of the local legal paper in your area.

Tip

One of the problems with checking these notices (as well as the notices filed with the county clerk) is that they tend to give the "legal description" of the property. Instead of 32 Johnson Drive, they may give a tract, block, and map number. Unless you're able to read recorded maps, such information isn't all that helpful.

There is an alternative. Usually advertised in legal newspapers are private listing companies which, for a fee, will sell you a list of properties in foreclosure, giving their common street address. Be aware, however, that frequently this list is costly, often more than $100 a month. (Which is why it's nice to have a friend at a title insurance company who can get you such a list for free!) If you find it useful, just call up and subscribe to these lists as you would to any other service.

Finally, each savings and loan, bank, and other lender has a foreclosure department (not to be confused with an REO department, to be discussed shortly). The foreclosure department handles delinquent mortgages. Making a friend there, one who is willing to share the lender's list with you, can prove to be a very wise and profitable move.

Stage Two—Buying at Foreclosure Sale

When the seller runs out of time, the property is sold "on the courthouse steps" to the highest bidder. Of course the main bidder at this sale is the lender, who bids the amount of the mortgage plus penalties and unpaid interest.

However, this is a public sale and anyone, including you, can bid. Sometimes the very best bargains are picked up at foreclosure sales.

Tip

Typically, such sales are for all cash. That means that you will have to arrange for any financing you need well in advance. To bid at this sale you will need to alert the trustee or court, come in with a certified check usually for a substantial portion of the winning price, and agree to come up with the balance within a few days at most. Most investors who bid at foreclosure sales have cash available to them. (They refinance later, once they have bought the property.)

Trap

Buying at a foreclosure sale is like shooting blind. There are no guarantees or warranties. For example, a trustee may be selling a property at a foreclosure sale where the loan amount is $20,000. If you bid $20,100 you may win. But *what* do you win?

You may not end up with clear title to the property. If the loan was a second mortgage, for example, you may find that a first mortgage is already in place. It could be for $175,000. Therefore, your $20,100 investment bought you a property with an existing $175,000 mortgage on it.

Of course, if the property is worth $300,000, you got a great deal. But if it turns out to be worth only $100,000, in retrospect the deal won't look good at all.

Buying at a foreclosure sale should really be attempted only by experienced real estate investors. You will need to thoroughly investigate the title to be sure of what other liens (mortgages) are on the property. And you will probably need a good real estate attorney's help to be sure that you end up with clear title.

My advice is to *stay away* from stage two foreclosure sales if you are just getting started. Their appeal is the possibility of getting a property at a terrific price. But the chance of losing money is so great for the novice investor that, in my opinion, it far outweighs the profits to be made.

Stage Three—Buying an REO

REO stands for "real estate owned." It represents the homes and other properties that lenders have taken back by foreclosure. Often these are then resold at steep discounts, and thus make for potentially great investments.

However, it can be difficult to locate these REOs. To understand why, you have to remember that for a financial officer in a lending institution, R-E-O are the three letters he or she dislikes hearing the most.

Lending institutions, and in particular S&Ls, are in business primarily to make loans and collect interest. They need to collect that interest in order to pay out interest on deposits, and hence to remain solvent. As a result, the most important officer in a lending institution is the one who makes loans, *good* loans. (A good loan is one that the borrower repays on time.) A lending officer who makes good loans can be highly rewarded.

In recent times, however, with falling real estate prices and recession, many borrowers have been unable to make their mortgage payments. The lenders have foreclosed. The property that's taken back is then given to a different kind of bank employee, an REO officer. Mortgages are considered assets, but REOs are considered liabilities. Hence, it is the REO officer's job to get rid of these properties as soon as possible.

There are always REOS on the market. It is an exceptional lender that doesn't have any. Most are always processing a few.

However, when the market turns down in real estate, the number of borrowers who don't pay increases. In recent years lenders have been holding and trying to dispose of great numbers of REO properties. (The job of the Resolution Trust Corporation—RTC—which has been much in the news as of this writing, is to get rid of REOs from insolvent banks and S&Ls. Most of these, however, are larger commercial properties.)

You would think that lenders would be stumbling over themselves trying to find buyers for their REOs. That, however, is not the case. Almost universally, lenders won't admit publicly that they even have an REO problem. Most won't even admit they have any REOs! Their reasoning is that to do so would cause the public to lose confidence in them. And that could lead to their demise. Thus, although REOS can be an excellent investment opportunity for you, it can be difficult to find out about them.

What you have to do is to contact the lenders directly. Basically you need to let a lender know that you are a *sophisticated* investor. You need to let the lender know that you understand what an REO is and that you'd like to bid on one.

Once the lender understands that you're a real investor, it may open up, in a limited sort of way.

For example, I recently called up the main offices of a large lender in the San Francisco bay area. I asked to talk to the officer in charge of the REO department. For a few minutes the operator seem confused. They had a loan department, an escrow department, an operations officer. She didn't have an REO department listed.

I asked to talk to the operations officer. (The operations officer handles day-to-day operations of the lending institution.) I explained to her that I was an investor and wanted to speak to someone in the REO department. I was given a number to call.

When I called the number I explained that I was an investor interested in purchasing an REO. Could I get a list of REOs available from the lending institution?

No, I was told. No such list existed. (I found it very hard to believe that the lender didn't have a list of its own properties.) I understood that to the REO officer, I was just a voice on the end of the line. Someone unknown, to whom the officer wasn't about to release information considered delicate. So I tried a different approach.

I said I was looking for REOs in a particular area. I gave the community, a rather small district of the city. Did the S&L have any REOs in that area?

There was a pause, and then the officer was saying that yes, there were three. If I was interested in them I could come down and fill out an identity form, and they would then give me the addresses so I could go out and look them over.

Tip

Don't limit yourself to one lender. Attempt to contact the REO officer at many lending institutions. Each will have a different set of rules. Some will exclude you. Others will be happy to talk with you. Play the odds. You're likely to get through to several.

Sometimes when you call a lender you will be told that all their REOs are listed with local real estate agents. The agents handle the sale for the lender, who has no direct sales to the public.

Fine. Deal with the agent.

I have bought REOs through agents, and it can work out well. Typically a lender will designate a particular broker to handle all its REOs in an area. Usually it is one of the larger and more active offices.

Just call up the office and ask to speak to the agent who handles the REOs for "XYS" S&L. Usually there is one agent who does this, although in large offices sometimes all the agents "co-broke" or work on REO sales.

Talk to the agent. Explain you're an investor looking for a good REO deal. Get to know the agent a bit, and allow him or her to get to know you.

Typically you will be told that the agent doesn't have any REOs from the S&L *at the present time*. The reason is quite simple. These are good deals, and they sell quickly. Just ask to be put on the list.

Tip

Don't rely on someone else's list. Call back frequently to be sure you're still being considered.

Sold "As Is"

One of the problems with REOs is that they are often in distressed condition. Consider if you were the borrower and were losing the house, your equity, your credit rating—would you be anxious to keep watering the lawn or to clean up when you left?

Most borrowers who lose their property through foreclosure not only do not clean up, they actually go out of their way to mess up the property. Their reaction, naturally enough, seems to be one of anger, and since they really can't take it out on anyone personally, they typically take it out on the property. Therefore, most REOS are a real mess.

However, many times lenders will fix up the REOs themselves. They know that a distressed property will get them a distressed price. On the other hand, if they fix it up, they stand to get a far better price.

The problem with fixing it up in a down market, however, is that since sales volume is so low, a lender may have to wait months to get a good price even after the property has been fixed up. In their desperation to get the REO off the books, they may decide to sell it immediately, "as is," for far less.

Offer to take the property off the lender's hands "as is." Of course, your price will be lower. But you're offering a quick sale. That's something that will catch the lender's ear.

Tip

If possible, also offer all cash. That will mean it's a clean deal and the lender is out of it. This will help to motivate the lender to agree to your price.

To get all cash, arrange financing elsewhere with another lender.

Trap

Sometimes properties are so run-down that no other lender will finance them. Be sure to check around first before offering cash. If no other lenders will handle the property, you will have to ask the REO lender to take back a mortgage. Most will do so in such circumstances.

Check Out the Property

If you find a distressed REO that otherwise fits your needs in terms of location, tenant market, etc., be sure to carefully calculate the combined cost of fixing it up.

You may have to call out a painter, plumber, and electrician. (In truth, to be successful, you're going to have to eventually make contact with "handymen" who can do this for you, or you're going to have to learn how to do it yourself.) You may have to calculate the cost of having someone come in and clean out the mess. You'll have to calculate re-landscaping costs, and so forth.

Trap

Often distressed properties are in distressed neighborhoods. Remember to judge the neighborhood first and foremost. Don't become enraptured by visions of refurbishing the house until you're convinced that the neighborhood warrants it. If there's a high crime and vandalism rate in the neighborhood, you may find that as fast as you clean up and fix up there's someone coming around to tear down and mess up. That's a hopeless situation, one of the worst, and you want to avoid it at all costs.

Make an Offer a Lender Can't Refuse

Once you've done your homework in determining that the REO is a good prospect in terms of location, rental market, and so forth, and you've determined the total cost of bringing it into rentable shape, calculate what you're going to offer the lender. Keep in mind that everything in real estate, especially including an REO, is negotiable.

Tip

Good REO property is in high demand by investors. Keep in mind that there may be many offers on the house you are considering. The lender, naturally enough, is going to accept the best. As a consequence, you need to make your offer as sweet as possible, without hurting yourself.

As noted earlier, if possible offer cash. Lenders love cash. (Of course, you're financing with another lender.) If you can't offer terms, offer a higher price with terms. Offer as much as possible (while allowing yourself a margin for profit after fix-up and cleanup). But insist on terms that you can live with.

For example, you may ask the lender to make a 90 percent loan on that full purchase price, at a favorable interest rate.

Tip

You can sweeten the pot by offering a short period of time for the loan, say two to five years. This allows you time to fix up, rent, and resell or refinance. But more important, it guarantees the lender that it will be out of the property after a set amount of time.

Don't hesitate to ask for a "fix-up/cleanup" allowance. This simply means that the lender will give you cash back out of the new mortgage (typically made in payments as the work is completed) to do the work.
Ask the lender to pay its share of normal closing costs, even as you offer to pay yours. You can ask the lender to pay *all* closing costs, but this sours the deal a bit.

Trap

Be aware that if make an offer that is accepted by a lender, you will be committed. You'll be expected to put down the agreed-upon down payment and go through with the deal. However, in my own experience, I have not come across a lender who would sue a buyer who didn't perform. Lenders, however, will not hesitate to keep your deposit if you default on your agreement to purchase.

Anytime you buy anything "as is," expect the unexpected. That's doubly the case with an REO. You can't always determine all of the problems with a property in a brief inspection. With a house and a normal seller, there will be disclosures. With a lender, there may not be. (A lender may simply disclose that it has no knowledge of any defects—that may be true, but it won't help you.)

Trap

Be sure that you stipulate that the property must be vacant when you take possession. Otherwise a nonpaying tenant may be inside, and you'll have to go through the costly eviction process.

REO's can be great deals. I've have good luck with many of them. But they take hunting to find, patience to fix up, and a bit of luck to sell at a profit.

11
Buying at Auction

Auctions have appeared around the country with increasing regularity, to help dispose of property from single-family homes to huge shopping centers. The allure of these auctions is the chance to buy at a greatly reduced price. The danger is that you'll pay too much, or get a property that has a serious defect.

In general, most auctions buyers I've talked to have been satisfied. They feel they have gotten a fair price and, in some cases, a terrific price. Unfortunately, that's not always the case.

What Are Auctions?

Auctions as a means of selling a commodity are not new. They're ancient. They are a tried and true method of selling dating back to the bazaars of ancient Mesopotamia.

In an auction, ancient or modern, owners of commodities—whether they be jars of olive oil, slaves, or real estate—consign their wares to an auctioneer. The auctioneer, a person skilled in dealing with crowds, has told the owners that he can sell their merchandise for them and get a good price for it. They trust him. They put themselves in his hands.

Modern real estate auctions are frequently advertised with full-page ads in major newspapers. There also may be an expensive, colorful brochure describing the property, and on the day of the auction, treats and champagne may be served to the bidders!

But don't be confused by the glamour and glitter. It's still the sale of a property, and if you're an investment buyer, you need to follow the same rules: Check out the property, figure out the maximum you can afford, and don't pay too much.

The subject of auctions is quite broad, and is dealt with in detail in a separate chapter of *The McGraw-Hill Real Estate Handbook*, Second Edition. However, here are some things to watch out for.

Reserves

A "reserve" means that there is a minimum price below which the seller will refuse to sell. (Sometimes the reserve amount is not announced.)

In reality most sales are reserve sales. Few sellers are willing to take a chance that due to freak circumstances, such as poor weather causing a low turnout, or competition from other sales, or little interest in the auction, there will be only a few low bids.

What this means, therefore, is that when you go to one of these auctions, you may not be able to get a "steal." Any really low price can be rejected by the seller as being below the reserve.

Tip

The seller doesn't have to honor the reserve. If it appears that there has been strong bidding on the property, but bidders really don't feel it's worth as much as the reserve, the seller may opt to take the highest bid below the reserve. I've seen this happen several times. (Usually, however, it's not done right at the time of the auction. Rather, the seller contacts the highest bidder and says, "If you'd still like to take the property at your highest bid, it's yours.")

Trap

Beware of sales where nothing is said about a reserve. In a straightforward auction the auctioneer will announce that there is a reserve, although he or she may not spell out exactly what it is.

Absolute Auctions

Here it is announced beforehand that there is *no* reserve. The highest bid takes the property, no matter what the price may be.

You may get a better deal at an absolute auction. But just remember, you're not likely to be the only one who thinks so. There may be a lot of people out there hoping to get a steal just like you, and together you could force the price up higher than it really should go. Sometimes absolute auctions get higher prices than reserve auctions!

Trap

Beware of phony "absolute" auctions. Auctioneers are well aware that the number of buyers who show up at an absolute auction is often larger than is the case at a reserve auction. Consequently a few unscrupulous sellers may falsely advertise such a sale when it isn't so.

There is supposed to be no reserve, yet when the bidding is low, it always seems that there are a couple of people (usually the same ones) in the audience who bid the prices higher. As a result, no properties go for really low prices.

Using "shills" in the audience to artificially keep prices up is illegal in most states. Many states even have written laws that prohibit the seller or his agents from bidding on property at an absolute auction. In actual practice, however, it's very hard to prove that someone is acting in this way.

However, if you're at an auction where you want to bid, and the same two people keep chiming in whenever prices are low and bid it up, you can be pretty sure that some sort of hanky-panky is afoot. I would simply pick up and get out of there. You won't get a deal at an unfair auction, no matter what you do.

Just remember, these unfair auctions are in the small minority. Most are run fairly by legitimate companies.

The Draw of the Spectacle

As noted earlier, beware of all the hoopla that often goes along with an auction. It may be held in a beautiful white tent with balloons and streamers. There may be free food, and wine- tasting. (It should go without saying that you should never drink intoxicating beverages while you're conducting real estate or any other kind of business.)

The auctioneer and his or her associates may be dressed in tuxedos. The whole thing may have an "upscale event" beat to it.

Don't be fooled. The atmosphere has been carefully orchestrated to create a "group mentality" calculated to make you loosen your wallet and to think you're getting a great deal when you're not. It still all comes back to dollars and common sense. The auctioneers can put a washed face on it but it's still a hard sell, and you'd be wise to always keep one hand on your wallet.

The Sale Itself

Most auctions require that you show up with a certain amount of cash or credit in order to bid. You may have had to fill out a form and submit to a credit check. Or you may need a cashier's check, typically made out to the auction company, for a set amount.

Once you bid and are successful, you will be expected to immediately turn over that check, or present cash or money in other form, as a deposit. You also will be required to execute a sales agreement and apply for a mortgage, usually through a lender of the seller's choice.

There's nothing wrong with any of this, as long as you realize up front that if you win the auction and then don't complete the sale, you may lose your deposit. Further, you don't have all of the opportunities to back out that you might have with a conventional sale.

When you buy at an auction, you're usually stuck with the property. (Just another reason to be sure to check it out beforehand, and to bid only as much as you have determined is your maximum profitable amount.)

Trap

When you execute a purchase agreement, you may be agreeing to all the terms the seller wants. Be sure that you carefully read everything you sign, and be sure you understand it.

Tip

Most auctions are still subject to the real estate laws of your state. If things don't work out as you had been told they would and you feel you are being cheated, you can contact your state's real estate licensing board and seek redress.

Perhaps the greatest pitfall with buying at an auction is that, unless you're very knowledgeable about real estate, you can be at the mercy of what the auctioneer says. You may need the help of a competent real estate attorney, but you may not have one around when you are required to sign papers that commit you to making a deal or coming up with money.

My suggestion is that unless you're very knowledgeable, you be careful of auctions. Or hire an attorney or someone whose knowledge and experience you trust, to accompany you and advise you on everything from bidding to signing a purchase agreement.

Trap

Don't rely on the advice of the seller or the auctioneer. They aren't in your corner.

12

Avoiding Nasty Tax Surprises

The subject of real estate taxes, like any U.S. taxes, is complex and sometimes filled with gray, unclear areas. Some have even said that it's arcane.

Nevertheless there are specific rules that you must follow when you own investment property. These rules include such things as the length and type of depreciation you may use, the sorts of things you can deduct as expenses, and the way the tax is calculated.

Therefore, it should go without saying that you should seek competent tax advice both before, during, and after owning property. (Neither the author nor the publisher of this book is engaged in giving tax advice. See your own accountant, tax attorney, or other competent tax advisor for advice on real estate taxation.)

There are, however, at least two areas that can sometimes surprise investors, particularly those new to the world of real estate and income taxation. We'll cover both of these in a general way in this chapter. The idea here is to alert you to potential problems so that you can seek out information specific to your property from your own tax advisor.

The Active/Passive Surprise

Most people have heard of the wonderful tax "write-offs" that real estate offers, or at least used to. Stories of investors who were able to reduce their personal income virtually to zero by investing in "tax-sheltered" real estate still abound amongst those new to the field.

As more experienced investors know, however, all that changed back in 1986 with the Tax Reform Act. That act created three categories of investment, two of which, active and passive, we're concerned with here.

All regular personal income was defined by the Act as active. That included income from wages, self-employment, and so on. All real estate was defined as passive.

The rule that changed real estate was that losses from passive income could not be written off against losses from active income. To see how this operates, let's use an example.

Harriet bought an investment house. Her total annual income from rents, less vacancies, was $11,000. Her total expenses, however, including mortgage interest, taxes, insurance, maintenance, repairs, and depreciation was $16,000. Harriet's property lost $5,000 a year.

Total income	$11,000
Total expenses	16,000
Loss	5,000

In the old days, before the 1986 Tax Reform Act, Harriet could have written off that $5,000 against her ordinary income. If she had wages, she could, in effect, have deducted the $5,000 from her total wage income.

After 1986, however, she could not. (We'll get to the exception shortly.) The $5,000 loss was carried forward and could be offset by a gain on other passive income, say a gain on the sale of another piece of real estate. Or it would finally be resolved as a loss (or gain) against ordinary income when she eventually sold the property. In short, even though Harriet lost money on the property, she couldn't write off that loss annually.

This has been an enormous surprise to many new investors going into real estate. While losses are often largely just on paper, coming from depreciation, many times they are also out-of-pocket. Even before depreciation, some properties show losses due to heavy maintenance and repair costs, or because rents are too low to pay for mortgage interest, taxes, and insurance.

It's a nasty surprise to realize in April that all those bucks you've been paying out of your pocket over the last year, to keep up that rental property, aren't even deductible!

Tip

There is an exclusion for low- to moderate-income property owners. If your personal income is less than $100,000, you can in fact write off against it (active income) up to $25,000 in loss from passive rental properties.

Between $100,000 and $150,000 income, you lose that exclusion at the rate of 50 cents for each dollar of higher income. For example, at an income of $125,000 your maximum exclusion is $12,500. At $150,000, it's zero.

If you feel that you qualify for this exclusion, don't rely on the short summary given above. There are some strict requirements that must be met. Check with a competent tax advisor. It could save you a bundle of money!

The No-Big-Capital-Gain-Rate Surprise

Many beginning small investors in real estate indeed do qualify, income-wise, for the exclusion noted above. That means that they will be able to write off the loss from their rental property, at least in part, against their ordinary income. However, that leads to another potentially nasty surprise.

A large part of the write-off from rental real estate is always depreciation. Here's a quiz for you. Let's assume you've purchased a rental home for $100,000, and you are able to use the exclusion to write off $3,500 a year in depreciation from your ordinary income. Further, let's assume that you've kept the property for nine years and then sold it for $140,000, using an agent who charges a 6 percent commission, and have $4,600 in additional closing costs. What's your profit, gain, and tax?

Quiz	
Purchase price	$100,000
Sales price	140,000
Agent's commission	8,400
Other closing costs	4,600
Depreciation (9 years)	31,500

For most of us, profit means subtracting the sales price from the purchase price, less costs of sale. If you answered $27,000 ($140,000 less commission, closing costs, and purchase price), you're correct. That's your profit. But that may not be what you put into your pocket.

Now, what's your gain?

If you answered $27,000 again, you're wrong. "Gain" is a technical term used by the government to determine how much of the sale is taxable. Your gain is actually $58,500.

Calculating Gain	
Sales price	$140,000
Less basis in property (purchase price less depreciation)	68,500 (100,000 − 31,500)
Less costs of sale	13,000
Total taxable gain	58,500

Note: For explanatory purposes, we are making this calculation some-what differently from the way the government would like to see it made.

Trap

The actual cash you will receive back in the above example is $27,000. However, you will pay tax at roughly the ordinary income rate on the taxable gain of $58,500. Assuming a combined federal and state income tax rate of 40 percent (it will vary depending on your other income and the state in which you live), your actual tax could be $23,400. After pay-ing taxes, your net cash out of the above sale would (roughly) only be $3,600!

What's happened is that, over the nine years that you've owned the property, you qualified for the exclusion noted earlier and wrote off $3,500 in depreciation each year. That lowered your taxable income by $3,500 in each of those years, and enabled you to pay less in taxes. When you sold, however, all of that depreciation came back at you and you had to pay in taxes all that you had saved (and perhaps more, depend-ing on your tax rate).

This is the biggest nasty surprise that people who have owned real es-tate for some time have been experiencing of late. It's also the reason that many real estate investors are hanging on to their properties rather than selling. They're hoping that the government will once again insti-tute a capital gains tax rate.

With a Capital Gains Tax Rate

In the past (prior to 1986) when the capital gains tax also was elimi-nated, when you sold property you had held for some time you were taxed at a much lower tax rate. Instead of paying income at the ordinary rates, you paid it at a much lower rate, perhaps half as much as the ordinary rate. This was called the "capital gains tax rate." It immensely benefited those who own and sell real estate (as well as stocks and other capital investments). In those days, real estate was actually a vehicle for converting cash from ordinary rates to a lower capital gains rate.

As of this writing, however, the capital gains tax rate is only history. Without it, that depreciation comes back at you as ordinary income and can wipe out part or even all of the profit you hope to receive from your investment property.

That's an excellent reason why you should consult with your tax adviser even before you purchase investment property. You may want to structure the purchase in such a way as to reduce the taxes you will eventually need to pay.

Note: We are talking here strictly about *investment* real estate, not your principal residence. Different rules apply to residences.

Trap

With a principle residence, you may be able to "roll over" your gain by replacing your old home with a new one, within certain time limits. This means you may not need to pay tax in the year of the sale. This does not apply to investment property, however. It's important not to get the two confused. Remember, the rules for a principal residence are different from those on investment real estate. See your tax adviser for more details.

Tip

Because of the way the tax laws are currently structured, two strategies may be in order. You may want to buy and sell quickly, if possible. In so doing depreciation will not be a major factor.

Or you may want to buy and hold long-term. Eventually there's a chance that the government will put a capital gains tax rate back on the books. (It makes good economic sense.) If you're considering this second alternative, I suggest you check into the book *Buy, Rent, and Hold*, McGraw-Hill, 1991, by my favorite author.

Appendix

Converting Negative Cash Flows to Positive

One of the underlying principles outlined in this book is that we should always aim at purchasing properties that will yield a positive cash flow. In other words, once we buy the property, we want it to make money for us, not lose it.

Occasionally, though, our judgment errs. What looked good on paper ends up being not quite so good in fact. We may end up with a property that costs us money. In a mild case, we could find ourselves paying a hundred dollars or so out of our pockets each month in addition to rental income to keep the property going (pay the mortgage, taxes, insurance, maintenance, etc.). In a worst-case scenario, the amount can run up to many hundreds of dollars a month or even thousands of dollars a month out of pocket. This latter kind of property is called an "alligator"—it eats us up alive with its costs.

If we end up with a negative cash flow property, recriminations won't help. We can blame our spouse, our agent, our lender, the seller, or (in rare cases) even ourselves for the bad situation. But doing that usually doesn't make things any better. What we need are methods of turning that negative cash flow property around so that at worst we reduce the money hemorrhage to a manageable flow and at best we turn it into a positive.

Following are 11 methods for converting a negative to a positive cash flow. Certainly not all will work for every property. Even if only one works for you, however, it will be a godsend.

1. Take Over Management of Property

If you are using a property manager, the first thing you should consider doing is taking back the control of your property.

Just doing so might turn your negative cash flow around. For example, if you're paying a property manager $100 a month, when you take over management, that's suddenly a $100 monthly expense that stops. This may make a big difference in itself.

Secondly, there's the matter of repairs and maintenance. With a property manager, almost certainly these were hired out and chances are the rates were fairly high. In the past I've used property managers and I've found that the fees they charged for maintenance, though reasonable given the marketplace, were far higher than if I handled the problem myself. In one case, when a light switch went bad, the property manager sent out an electrician. Cost of the switch—99 cents. Cost of the electrician—$65. My cost to fix it would have been about a dollar.

Or when the stove had a problem, a plumber was sent. Parts to clean a burner—35 cents in detergent. Labor—$55. Again, my costs would have been negligible.

The property manager, of course, was only doing the job "by the book." For plumbing problems, hire a plumber. For electrical problems, hire an electrician, and so forth. In many cases, however, a "handyman" (yourself) can do the same work for a fraction of the cost.

When I discussed this with one property manager, she pointed out that there was also the question of liability to consider. What if she sent a handyman to fix a gas stove and the work was done improperly? The stove might catch fire or explode. What if the switch was wired improperly? She simply couldn't risk the liability.

If you do the maintenance yourself, the liability argument remains. If you work on the electrical or gas system of a house and something should go wrong, you could be held liable.

Nevertheless, in my own houses, I don't hesitate to clean the stove or replace a light switch. Most homeowners do the same. I feel I'm competent to do those things. (You may not be. I'm not recommending that you do anything you aren't competent to handle.)

The point is, when you do it yourself, you save money, a lot of money.

One property manager I hired charged me $100 for cleaning the screens on a house. The screens were cleaned, but I later did a similar job myself on another house in an hour with a hose!

Not that I'm down on property managers. I'm not. But if your property is producing negative cash flow, you need to quickly look at areas where you can turn it around. Taking over the management yourself can be one of the fastest ways.

Remote Properties

A big problem with taking over the management of property is frequently its distance. If you're in California and your rental units are in Arizona, you're hard pressed to remove your property manager. After all, you can't be Johnny-on-the-spot to fix a maintenance problem or show the property to a prospective tenant. Hopping on a plane every day to attend to a distant residential property obviously isn't feasible. So what do you do if you have property that's some distance away?

The answer here is simple. You don't buy property that is more than 30 miles away from home. If you do have property that's far away, sell it. Distant property with a negative cash flow is hopeless. There's no way to turn it around. Dump it.

2. Dump the Loser

As noted above, property that is far away and that has negative cash flow, in my opinion, should be sold. But what about properties that are close to home? Is there a similar reason for selling them?

Yes. But it's important to first identify those properties that are hopeless losers and should be dumped. With those far away it's easy. With those close by, it can be harder.

That's not to say that a close-in property with a significant negative cash flow is hard to identify. If we have a condo on which we are losing $300 month after month when it's fully rented, we have a loser. (Of course, in the old days that loss might have been written off against our taxes. But today, we may not be able to do that so easily. Remember, passive activities can't be written off against our income, except for the exclusion.)

In most cases, identifying a property to sell isn't hard. Sell any with big negative cash losses that aren't rapidly appreciating in value.

It's a bit trickier with close-in properties that are marginal. These are the properties that seem to have great potential. Yet for one reason or another, they just never turn around.

One investor friend had a property that, when it was rented, showed a positive cash flow. But for some reason it was difficult to keep rented. Most tenants only stayed a few months before they moved out.

It took the owner a relatively short time to rerent, usually two or three weeks. But she was losing those two or three weeks' worth of rent three or four times a year. That was the equivalent of having the place vacant almost a full two months annually. The result was that on an annual basis the property showed a huge negative cash flow, although on a month-to-month basis when rented, it had a positive cash flow.

The owner tried everything. She insisted on leases from tenants. In those cases the tenants, after a few months, broke the leases.

What was the problem? It could have been bad neighbors. It could have been something intrinsically wrong with the design of the house. It could simply have been bad luck.

It really didn't matter what the problem was. That there was a problem with the property was enough. In this case the owner found it impossible to write off the loss. The property was not appreciating rapidly. Thus there was only one solution for her—dump the property. That's just what she did.

Today, investors simply don't have time to try to turn a problem property around. The downside to almost any property comes up too fast. As soon as we identify a loser, we should dump it.

Selling at a Loss

The problem with selling, of course, is that frequently the house or condo that's the loser is the one that is most difficult to sell. It may be a depressed area where prices are falling or it may have features that detract from its value. When we try to sell, we may find that we can only do so if we take a loss. Should we sell at a loss just to dump the loser?

That depends on several factors, among them:

How much is our negative?

How much would we lose in a sale?

Can we economically and psychologically afford to lose money each month?

The first two calculations are relatively simple. Just find out what the property would sell for by contacting brokers in the area, subtract costs of sale, and that gives you your answer. If you get net cash out, don't hesitate. If you're "upside down" and you owe more than the house is worth, consider selling anyway. You may be able to deduct the capital loss.

But, if you're way "upside down," take a longer look at the property. Calculate your negative cash flow for the next five years on the property. Figure in what you think will happen in the area. Will prices turn around? Will you be able to sell for a profit five years down the road?

If you lose less by selling now than by holding for five years, you may want to bite the bullet and sell. The property is a real dog and you're probably better off without it.

On the other hand, if you lose more by selling than you would by holding for five years, you may want to reconsider. Remember, during that time, chances are you'll be able to increase rents somewhat. And if expenses stay constant, you could be working your way toward positive cash flow.

Finally, there's the psychological drain of losing money each month. Can you handle writing checks out of your personal income each month to keep the property going, even if you can afford it? Many people simply cannot: They find it brutally oppressive.

If that's the case with you, then I suggest you forget the economic considerations and get rid of the property at any cost.

From a strategic perspective, dumping a loser is not a good way to handle real estate. It means admitting a mistake was made. It often means taking a loss. But it may be better to admit the mistake and take the loss than to continue on hopelessly with a negative cash flow.

3. Get a Positive Property to Offset a Negative One

Under the current tax rules, all real estate is passive. That means, as noted, that we can't write off real estate against our regular income. But it also means that we can write off real estate losses against real estate gains. This provides an opportunity for some investors.

If you have a property that has a negative cash flow, one way of offsetting it is to obtain another property with a positive cash flow. The negative can be used to offset the positive so that we achieve at least a break-even.

This is a simple solution that is not quite so simple to accomplish. To begin with, we don't want this solution to precede the "dump the loser" solution noted above. My suggestion is that if you have a loser you can't tolerate, you dump it. You don't first try to offset the loss with a winning property.

On the other hand, if you have a property that has a small negative cash flow, and you feel that the property will eventually turn around, then you may very well want to try to offset the loss with another, winning, property.

Quite frankly, it's not impossible to find a property that will give you a positive cash flow. The prospects for offsetting a loser with a winner, in most areas, are actually fairly good.

When to Offset a Loser with a Winner

What this recommendation involves is putting good money in after good. If you already have a property, then chances are you put in some of your cash to get it. It may be a property with good appreciation potential. In such a case, sticking in more money to buy a second positive cash flow property makes excellent sense. All that you are doing is protecting your investment.

4. Trade the Investment Property

This is an alternative that surprisingly few people consider. But it makes excellent economic sense. There are good reasons for trading:

1. When we sell, we get all the taxable gain hitting us. When we trade, however, it's normally possible to defer any gain onto the next property. There are distinct tax advantages to trading over selling. (Note: There are very specific rules and requirements for trading real estate. Be sure to check with a specialist in the field before beginning any trade.)

2. Often we can trade a property to avoid selling at a loss.

Let's say we own a home that is losing $400 a month. We want to dump this loser in the worst possible way. However, if we sell, by the time we pay closing costs and lower our price sufficiently to find a buyer, we may take a beating.

On the other hand, we offer to trade. We find someone who has a small residential lot somewhere with just about the same equity as we have in the house. This person is looking for a house that they may later want to convert to a residence. We make a trade and we get the lot. We get full price, they get full price. (One of the nice things about a trade is that the price stops being such a stumbling block. Traders are more concerned about equities.)

Since the lot is paid off, we don't have any negative (except for taxes, which are probably small). Eventually, if the lot isn't out in the desert or under water, it will probably be worth something. Consequently, what we've done, instead of taking an immediate loss, is project our investment into the future in such a way that there's no negative cash flow. In effect, we've buried our investment. We'll forget about it for a while and hope that eventually it may grow into something valuable.

Of course, trades made in heaven like this don't happen all the time. We may need a three-way trade to get what we want. We may end up with another property that's only a little bit better than the one we originally had and may need to trade again.

The point is that we won't know what we can trade for, until we try. Trading should be a realistic option to seriously consider.

How to Trade

If you haven't traded before, then you'll want to have the services of a trading broker the first time you do. Very few brokers regularly trade properties. Ninety-nine percent of all agents only handle sales. You'll want to ask several brokers for recommendations before you find a trader in your area.

Traders belong to trading clubs. They usually meet weekly, at which time they describe their listings and then write up tentative deals. Deals written on your property are really just offers to trade. When you list your property with a trading broker, you may find you have all kinds of crazy offers coming in—and some not so crazy, too. People may want to trade for boats, cars, diamond rings, or anything else. You may find that trading definitely expands your options. (One rule of a tax-deferred trade is that both properties must be of "like kind." Be careful and check with a good tax attorney before making any trade.)

I have found that trying to trade for out-of-area properties is more difficult. If you're in Kansas City and you want to trade for a property in Minneapolis, you may find the deal tough, though not impossible. Sometimes interstate trades do work out.

Trading should not be considered your first option. But it definitely is an option worth considering.

5. Take in a Partner Who Has Shelter Opportunities

Another option is to consider selling a portion of your negative cash flow property. Perhaps you can't write off the negative because you have a high regular income. On the other hand, there are people with lower incomes who are still able to write off real estate losses against other income. (Remember the $25,000 allowance.) Taking in a partner can benefit you.

How to Do It

The idea is that the partner buys some of your equity and pays a portion of the expenses. In exchange, the partner gets all the tax write-off. You get some of your cash out and stop having to worry about the negative cash flow. Both of you will divide the profits when the property is sold. In this case, because the partner may have more to offer than you do, you might well have to give him or her a bonus in the form of increased equity, but the arrangement should work out in the long run.

The real trick, of course, is finding the right partner. Initially, it's going to be mostly word-of-mouth. You'll want to keep in contact with many brokers, spreading the word around for what you need. You'll also want to contact accountants, financial planners, those who help investors with their taxes. They may provide leads, too.

Note: It's important to understand that when you find the right partner, you still have to set up a partnership arrangement that you, the partner, and the IRS will accept. Therefore, you will want to consult with a competent CPA or tax attorney.

6. Refinance

This solution is so simple that occasionally we forget about it. It is possible to refinance the debt on our property, thereby achieving smaller payments and eliminating negative cash flow. This is certainly so if interest rates are lower than they were during the time of purchase.

It pays to check this out. Generally speaking, a refinance will lower payments under the following conditions:

1. A longer term loan

2. A reduced interest rate

3. Several smaller loans combined

Taking these one at a time, a long-term loan makes sense *if* we already have a short-term loan *or* if we have held the property for some years. For example, by opting for a 30-year as opposed to a 15-year mortgage, we cut our payments by 15 percent. That may be the difference between negative and positive cash flow.

On the other hand, if we have held our property—for 10 years, say—we may have paid down a significant part of our original loan balance. Now when we refinance, even for the same interest rate, we should secure a lower monthly payment.

Finally, if we have a second and additional mortgages on our property, these are typically for a shorter term (often 3 to 15 years) and a higher interest rate than we could get on a new first mortgage. By getting a new 30-year first mortgage for the full amount of the other mortgages on the property, we may be able to significantly cut down our payments.

Refinancing may be an alternative to getting rid of negative cash flow. But it does have a downside. It's expensive.

Today, to refinance usually costs between 4 and 5 percent of the mortgage value. And that assumes there are no special costs such as termite-damage repair or other work on the property that the lender requires. If we borrow $100,000, we are talking about paying an additional $4,000 to $5,000 just for the refinance.

Of course, these costs usually are just tacked onto the mortgage amount (assuming we have sufficient equity in the property—normally a new first that's refinanced can't be for more than 80 percent of the appraised value).

Nevertheless, the costs of refinancing reduce our equity. When it finally comes time to sell at (hopefully) a profit, we will get our money out of the property *less the costs of obtaining the refinance* (assuming the costs were added to the mortgage).

Therefore, I always suggest a careful evaluation of our goals for the property. If we're planning to resell within the next three years, it may not pay to refinance even to get rid of a negative cash flow. The costs of the refinance could be too heavy. On the other hand, if we plan to keep the property long term, then refinancing may definitely be the way to go.

7. Renegotiate the Current Loan

Again this is a potential solution that most investors never consider. Most of us are simply convinced that once we take out a mortgage from a lender, negotiations are finished. A more realistic tack to take, however, is to keep in mind that negotiations never end. This particularly holds true for lenders in a down real estate market.

A few years ago a friend bought a condo in a growing area for rental purposes. Shortly afterward, though, oil prices started going down and oil companies, the hub around which the area was growing, closed down.

Almost overnight the area became economically depressed. People moved away. Businesses closed, and it became difficult to rent the property. Eventually, in order to keep his property rented, my friend had to reduce rents to the point where he had a $400 a month negative on the property. He wasn't able to deduct the loss immediately from his income, so he incurred a $400 out-of-pocket expense every month.

Naturally, he wanted to dump the property. And yet, however hard he tried, he could not sell or trade. The area was so depressed that no one wanted to take on his loser.

Finally, in desperation, he went to the lender, a savings and loan association. After half an hour of talking, he got past the floor personnel and was ushered into a back room where the vice-president in charge of real estate lending had an office. She was not happy to see him.

My friend explained his predicament. He was losing money on the property. Yes, he could keep it rented. But no, he could not do so at break-even. Unless he got some relief somewhere, he was going to have to let the property go into foreclosure.

The loan officer did not like to hear that. The S & L already had thousands of REO properties taken back because the owners could not make payments in the slumping housing market and poor overall economy. The S & L's very solvency was at stake.

Rather than take back another property, the loan officer suggested a compromise. The lender would restructure the mortgage and offer a lower interest rate at a longer term. The new interest rate was substantially below market.

As a result, my friend suddenly found that he could rent the property at break-even, which he is now doing. His hope is that eventually when the local economy turns around, as he's sure it will, he will be able to sell at a profit.

Not all lenders are willing to renegotiate. But these days, with parts of the economy in steep recession or even depression, some certainly are. You'll never know until you ask.

8. Give the Property Back

In number seven above, the suggestion was that the loan be renegotiated with the lender and the assumption was that the lender was an institution such as a savings and loan.

But what if the lender was the seller? Many times property is purchased through seller financing. What if the house or condo you want to dump because of severe negative cash flow was one financed by the seller?

My suggestion is that you see the former owner and explain the situation exactly as you see it. You may be having, for example, a $350 negative cash flow on the property. You cannot tolerate that. You explain the situation to the seller and offer to give the property back *if* the seller will return at least a portion of your down payment.

You can expect the former owner to laugh at this suggestion, *until* you point out that if he or she does not agree to this, you will simply stop making payments on the mortgage. You will continue to collect rents for the many months it takes for the former owner to foreclose on the mortgage. The former owner will go through the hassle and waste the time, not to mention spend the money out of pocket, that is required to foreclose on the property...*unless* the owner agrees to take it back and make some concessions.

At the very least, you may get the former owner to renegotiate the loan. Or the owner may be willing to take the property back and give you some financial consideration. Either way, for any propertery in this category, this is a viable option that definitely should be considered.

Deed in Lieu of Foreclosure

On the other hand, your lender may indeed be an institution such as an S&L that refuses to renegotiate the mortgage. What can you do then?

If you are so desperate as to be willing to give up your equity, you can offer to give the lender a deed to the property in lieu of foreclosure. It will save costs and you won't have the credit stain of a foreclosure on your record. (Be aware, however, that many lenders now report giving "deeds in lieu of foreclosure" to credit-reporting agencies.) For some investors this may be the only real solution.

Note: Giving a deed in lieu of foreclosure may not affect your credit rating in terms of getting bank loans or credit cards. But it could seriously affect your ability to get a new mortgage later on. Almost all lenders these days ask the following question on a mortgage application: "Have you ever given a deed in lieu of foreclosure?"

If you answer yes, you stand an excellent chance of having your mortgage application turned down. (You may be able to avoid a rejection by including a letter explaining extenuating circumstances with your new mortgage application.)

Of course, lying about giving a deed in lieu of foreclosure by answering no when you have indeed given such a deed is not a good idea. If the lender discovers the lie, which it very well may from a credit-reporting agency, it could be cause for refusing to give you the mortgage, for rescinding a mortgage already given, or for turning the matter over to authorities by reason of fraud.

9. Use a Lease Option

This is another way of removing negative cash flow from your property, but it has certain limitations that are important to understand.

In a "lease-option" the tenant is given the option of buying the property. Typically, the lease-option will call for the tenant to lease the property for two to three years. During that time a portion of each monthly payment will apply toward the down payment. At the end of the option period, *the tenant* can choose to buy the property or not. Let's take an example.

I have a house on which I am losing $200 a month. I am already at my maximum rental rate. So I now find a tenant who is willing to give me a lease option. I rent the property to the tenant for $200 a month more than my previous rental rate. Now I have achieved break-even, no negative.

Why is this tenant willing to pay a higher rental rate? The reason is that out of each monthly payment, I will credit, say, $300 toward the down payment. After three years, when the lease-option is up, the tenant will have a credit of $10,800. If the full down payment required to refinance is, for example, $15,000, the tenant now needs only to come up with $4,200 more plus closing costs.

Advantages

The advantages to me are twofold. First I have the property rented long term for enough money to break even. I've eliminated my negative cash flow. Second, I have at least a tentative sale. At the end of three years, the tenant hopefully will buy the property at a price we've agreed upon.

The advantages for the tenant are also twofold. First, he or she has locked in a price on a property three years in the future. Second, part of each month's rent is going toward the down payment

Disadvantages

The disadvantages to the tenant, however, are also twofold. First, under a lease-option the tenant is ordinarily expected not only to pay the rent but also to handle all the upkeep that normally would fall to an owner. This is an additional expense.

Second, the tenant is paying a higher than normal rent. Nothing wrong with this as long as the tenant follows through and makes the purchase, since a large portion of the monthly payment is going toward the down payment. But if the tenant does not or cannot fulfill the purchase, then paying the higher rent is going to waste.

The disadvantages to the landlord are threefold. First, if the tenant decides to purchase, you've given up part of your equity each month in order to achieve break-even. At purchase time you have to give the tenant a credit—in this case, $10,800—toward the purchase price.

Second, you've locked in a sales price three years ahead based on today's market. If the property goes up in value during the time, you don't benefit, the tenant-buyer does. (Some lease-options are written so that the sales price will be determined by independent appraisal at the time of purchase.)

Third, in *most* cases I've seen, the tenant doesn't exercise the option—never buys the property. In *most* cases, the tenant either cannot qualify for a new loan or cannot come up with the additional cash required for a down payment and closing costs.

Thus, to some extent, a lease-option is a kind of pipe dream for both tenant and landlord. The tenant thinks he or she is going to buy. The landlord thinks he or she has got a sale. But a few years down the road both suddenly discover that things just aren't working out as everyone thought they would.

Of course, this isn't always so terrible for the landlord. He or she has the property back after having received at least break-even for several years. It's a way of getting rid of a negative cash flow.

The potential problems are many, however. If halfway through the lease-option, the tenant realizes it isn't going to work out, stops taking care of the property, and, in the worst case, stops paying the rent, the landlord has a real hassle.

Fortunately, this worst-case scenario rarely happens. More often than not, after a year or so, if the tenant realizes that things are not going to work out, he or she will ask to be released from the lease. Most wise landlords, to avoid any possibility of damage to the property and of losing rent, will agree.

A lease-option, therefore, is a sometimes successful way out of negative cash flow. Yes, it can provide an excellent escape hatch when it works. But you have to keep in mind that it may only be a temporary solution.

10. Improve the Property to Increase Rents

Sometimes the reason a property will not produce the desired rent can be identified. Perhaps it's the carpeting. Our condo has old, stained, and torn carpeting. We can only get tenants by offering a lower rent. And the tenants we get tend to be the kind who don't take care of the place.

Or maybe we have a two-bedroom house and we are in a rental market where everyone has children and is looking for at least a three-bedroom house.

Or perhaps the property has large back and front yards that are weed-strewn. Prospective tenants take a look at the yards and decide they don't want the place.

Sometimes with a rental there will be a definable feature that is causing us to receive a reduced rent. The carpeting or the number of bedrooms or the yard is holding the property back. If only the problem were corrected, we could get enough rent to at least break even.

If the property has the potential to break even and if it doesn't cost too much for the improvement, my suggestion is to do the work. For example, new carpeting can be put into a rental for $12 a yard. Good-quality carpeting nowadays can be bought for $20 a yard. A 1,500-square-foot rental typically will require 130 yards to completely carpet (kitchen, baths, and closets frequently are left uncarpeted). That's a minimum expenditure of $1,560. It might be worthwhile in order to get a break-even rent.

Similarly, a garage might be inexpensively converted to an extra bedroom. If it can be done for a few thousand dollars, it too might be worthwhile in order to boost rents. (But check local building codes and deed restrictions in your area which may prohibit this.)

A sprinkler system and basic landscaping might cost $1,000. It might be well worth the money to get the higher rent.

The point is simple. Sometimes it pays to improve the property to get rid of a negative cash flow.

When It Doesn't Pay

A word of caution. Just improving the property may not necessarily guarantee higher rents. It probably will when there's a definable problem. But if the lower rent or the tenant problems are caused by other factors such as poor location or the age of the house, then no improvements may help.

It's important to carefully evaluate the property before spending money. Calling in a broker or a property manager as a consultant to get ideas may help. The rule is, improving properties with definable problems can improve cash flow. Improving properties where the problem is due to unalterable conditions is like throwing good money after bad.

11. Donate It to a Charity

Charitable donations are usually deductible. If you have a property that you can't get rid of any other way, that's pulling you down with negative cash flow, and that's in an area where appreciation seems unlikely, you may want to consider donating it to a church or other charitable organizations. It's unlikely that this will get you any cash out, but it may get you a deduction and you could be rid of the property.

The problem, of course, is getting a charity to take your property. If you own free and clear land or other property, it's usually no problem. Charities are eager to take over unmortgaged property. Their status means they probably won't have any property tax to pay and it becomes a positive "investment" for them.

If you have a mortgage, however, it's more difficult. First of all, the mortgage has to be assumable. (Charities have much difficulty getting new financing.)

Second, they must find a way to make money on the deal. Perhaps not having to pay taxes on the property will convert it from a negative cash flow to a positive one and they'll want to consider it. Giving up your equity may make it more alluring. Your previous relationship to the charity may also count.

In any event, if you're desperate, consider this as an alternative. But check with your tax advisor and accountant to be sure of the consequences for you.

These, then, are 11 possible solutions to negative cash flow problems. If you're burdened with out-of-pocket costs just to keep a property afloat, you may want to consider using one or more of them.

Index

About the Author

Robert Irwin has worked as a successful real estate broker for more than 25 years and has steered coutless buyers, sellers, and beginning investors through every kind of real estate investment imaginable. He has served as a consultant to lenders, investors, and other brokers and is one of the most knowledgeable and prolific writers in the field. His books include *Tips & Traps When Buying a Home; Tips & Traps When Selling a Home; Tips & Traps When Mortage Hunting; Buy, Rent, & Hold: How to Make Money in a "Cold" Real Estate Market; How to Find Hidden Real Estate Bargins;* and *The McGraw-Hill Real Estate Handbook,* Second Edition.